BOTH SIDES NOW

BOTH SIDES NOW

REFLECTIONS FOR WOMEN AT MIDLIFE

COLETTE M. TRACY

NEW DEGREE PRESS

BOTH SIDES NOW

Reflections for Women at Midlife

ISBN   979-8-88504-055-6   *Paperback*

             978-1-63730-389-4   *Kindle Ebook*

             978-1-63730-390-0   *Ebook*

To my brother Joe, whose contributions to my life are
evident in every page of this book. Forever, missed.

Contents

———

Introduction

———

A string of excited, fugitive, miscellaneous pleasures is not happiness; happiness resides in imaginative reflection and judgement, when the picture of one's life, or of human life, as it truly has been or is, satisfies the will and is gladly accepted.
—GEORGE SANTAYANA

For as long as I can remember, I have reflected on the seasons of my life. In addition, in my early adulthood I had pretty lofty goals, and had the blessing of achieving each one. That gave me my first feeling of being "invincible" and "in control," which seemed to be the mantra of my generation, at least that's what the music said. Then came my thirties, and reality hit hard. There was job loss (being let go), high risk pregnancies, and the loss of one of our babies when I was six months pregnant—a little girl who we named Julia.

Although it seemed impossible, life did go on. Mike and I were raising first born Ryan, and got pregnant again with my youngest, Ian. I spent the next twenty years working and raising a family. Then, one day it seemed I looked up and noticed that I was fifty. In the grand scheme of things today, forty, fifty, sixty, and even seventy are not old as long as we can stay active and healthy. When we reach this time in our lives it feels surreal, and many of us are saying, "How did I get here?"

I am one of those people who thought deeply about what my aunt was thinking about on her ninetieth birthday. I thought, *How do you feel knowing that you are nearing the end of life?* My aunt is totally amazing, and she has the vibrancy of someone much younger than her years. However, she says that she has lived a long rich life, but she is ready to go and see so many of her loved ones once again that have passed on. I remember as a preteen asking my parents, "What does it feel like to be old?" My parents said something so profound, I was always glad I'd asked. "If you are healthy, you never feel your age. We don't feel forty- and fifty-something. We still feel inside like we are twentyfive." What a great gift they gave me. It is no wonder they both lived to be in their nineties.

I remember when I was in my twenties I was hyperaware of what I observed in the culture of the eighties, where the pervasive message was above all else be independent, successful, ambitious, and driven. I married young, at twenty, but felt much pressure to have all the things I felt at the time were part of the mainstream middleclass. Therefore, as my husband recants with a tinge of regret, "All we did was work in our twenties." It was like I had this master plan. I had to have everything in place by the time I was thirty: married, check; college degree, check; owning a home, check; and pregnant by the time I was thirty, absolutely. By the time I turned thirty I did have all these things. Hence, the feeling that I was in control and my life was of my own creation.

I remember a book that I came across as an undergraduate while doing some sociology research; the book was called *The Singular Generation* by Wanda Urbanska. The book made a great impression on me as I felt Urbanska was spot on in her estimation of the lifestyles and attitudes of young people in the 1980s. According to Urbanska, it seems we were the most insecure generation due to the battle of the sexes—i.e., sexism, divorce—and the threat of nuclear war. And as a result we became the very first generation whose main involvement in life was almost a singular obsession with ourselves. The theme for the decade was acquisition, collecting as much material wealth as possible and keeping a sense of self and independence, regardless of whether one was in a so-called committed relationship.

Even for people like me that were in a very committed relationship and loved deeply, there was always this pervasive sense of doom that the relationship may fail, and there was a strong need to keep one's independence. I resonated with this. I remember my mother, not really understanding my need for education and independence, said to me, "It seems like you expect to be alone." I said to her, "How do I know that I won't be?" Additionally, there was always this sense of scarcity when it came to opportunity; we were the scavengers so to speak, with our noses pressed up against the glass. Thus, my need for control, planning, and thinking about what may lie around the corner was always a preoccupation of mine. Until very recently my mind was always focused on the future.

I think if most people see me today they would think that I have had a successful life, and for the most part I have; in the early years, however, my life was very difficult. For a time I suffered from crippling depression. I truly needed to reroute my life's path as for a couple of years I was not functioning. Yet through much hard work and the right support systems, I was able to overcome it very well. Again, to a large extent in my young adult years I still felt that "I" was in control of my life. The awakening in my mid-thirties was quite rude, to say the least, when I lost my baby girl to a stillbirth when I was six months pregnant. While I was strong, had an amazing family and friends, and never reverted to the extent of depression I had in my teens, I was diagnosed with PTSD.

An extremely difficult loss that I have more recently experienced is my brother, Joe. Joe and I were the best of friends. For our entire adult lives we spoke at least once a week and felt like we solved the world's problems through our many discussions about pop culture, gossip, business, politics, and of course our families. He was always there for me, and he was one of my biggest advocates and mentors. He was seven and a half years older than I was, so he always experienced everything first, and I always looked to him to show me the way.

About nine years ago, right after my dad passed away, Joe was having a difficult time because his son—his only child—was going off to college. My brother was always witty, and he was kind of dramatic in his humor. He said, tongue-in-cheek, "Well, my son's grown now. I'll be looking at retirement in a few years, and then all I'm waiting for is death." I remember laughing at him and saying, "Don't talk that way. You've got some amazing years still ahead of you." It kind of upset me because I knew a part of him was serious; but I also really thought about the fact that at midlife so many people may not say this, but it is surely how they feel. Less than ten years later, my brother passed away from pancreatic cancer.

Today, given some of the losses we have all experienced, it feels that it's enough for us to just be here in the moment, trying to make the most out of every day. Ageing in Western culture can be a difficult proposition. Those in middle age and beyond need to deal with not only potentially declining health, loss of employment, loss of spouse, loss of parents, and loss of loved ones and friends but also the need to face increasing scrutiny from a society that only values youth, beauty, and vitality. These mostly unattainable characteristics our culture expects from us affect women and men alike.

After the loss of a long-term job, the loss of my mother, and the loss of Joe, all over a three-year period, I told myself to stop living in and planning for the future—the future will be here soon enough. Especially as I think about getting older, how far in advance do I really want to focus? In fact, the best part of life now is trying to make the most out of every day with family, friends, and work. Resilience is such a great word, and one that I am hearing quite often today in these difficult times we are living in. Life is not easy, and it will not bend to our wills the way many of us felt it may have in years earlier. One of the most important things that I believe about getting older is we need to have resilience when it comes to dealing with changes and hard times.

Even though I know that I am strong, I know that there are things in life that can nearly destroy you if one doesn't look to a higher power for strength and guidance. In my opinion, it is always important to have faith; it becomes imperative as we age. Carl Jung, one of my favorite psychologists, believed that as people get to around midpoint in life, if they are healthy, there is a shift to a greater connection to a higher being—whether that is God, the universe, or a higher power—and that this connection is necessary for growth and maturation. I say we must believe in something more powerful than ourselves so we have a comforting place to go to when many of the people and places that we went to for shelter in our earlier lives may be gone.

The reason I feel I am the woman to write this book is because, although I still have my bad days, I have tapped into a faith that brings me a joy and peace (on many days, not all) that makes the world still a beautiful place that I feel privileged and grateful to be a part of. While I have been acutely aware of the changes going on in our world around me, I feel myself doing my best to make emotional adjustments as necessary. I have many passions, interests, and such a strong resolve to surround myself with the people and things that are most important to me. And while I know that I am not totally in control, I hope to align myself each day and live life for the higher purpose that I was made for. It seems like a tall order, I know. But like a colleague of mine said, "We're all just works in progress." While we are here, let's try our best to make the most out of it.

It is my fervent hope that through these stories about women, readers will learn and understand through their questions and answers how these women are living lives of resilience and creative transitions, and how these answers have brought them to a place of peace and well-being that wasn't necessarily there early on. I struggled with whether to write about women in midlife or women and men both. While I decided to make it more about the plight of women and what it's like to be a woman at midlife, I realize that men have their own challenges at this stage, but I believe that the lessons we learn in life about finding peace, love, and resilience are the same for us all. My goal is for women and men alike to understand the value, wisdom, and gift that comes with ageing. I want us to discover and link the common thread necessary to live a more hopeful, faithful, loving, and fulfilled life through all life's stages—particularly our later years.

CHAPTER 1

Change Your Mind, Change Your Life

Why do we, as a society and culture, scrutinize every aspect of a woman? When we look at women in our culture, we tend to examine and critique every part of her, searching for her imperfections. And as women, most of us are incredibly hard on ourselves. When we look for imperfections in other women, we are harsh and make comparisons; however, we are judging ourselves just as harshly. I've come to realize that the way we critique other women is the way we look at ourselves.

There are so many depictions in movies, videos, and music that ostracize women that don't fit a picture-perfect image. One of the movies that came out fairly recently that speaks about beauty and mind-set is *I Feel Pretty*. Amy Schumer plays Renee, depicted as an average size woman who feels that she and her life are "nothing special" at best. In the beginning of the movie it seems that everywhere she goes she is reminded of this. She views her life as boring and considers herself that dreaded word that so many of us don't like: average (Kohn & Silverstein 2019).

That is, until she has a small accident and hits her head. When Renee comes to, she sees herself in a totally new way—she sees herself as beautiful for the first time! I love the excitement and awe she feels and expresses when seeing herself as beautiful for the first time.

The first scene in the movie plays to Renee's insecurity with a shoe-size stereotype: she orders a pair of shoes at her gym for spin class, is embarrassed of her larger shoe size, and then the customer service person embarrasses her more by shouting out that she takes a double wide.

In one of the next scenes, we see Renee talking with her close friends about all the competition on a dating website and how she totally doesn't measure up. She talks about how all that matters is the picture, and how if you look great in your picture and you don't measure up in person the other person is disappointed and rejects you.

One of the obvious points to me in the movie is that we only feel as good about ourselves as we think we are. I remember even being in my thirties and still thinking that I paled in comparison to other women; and damn it, on paper (i.e., the right weight and body shape), there was no reason I should have felt this way. I remember telling this to my husband who replied, "No offense, but I find that hard to believe." The fact was I played the part and I had the goods—according to what Western society told us was attractive—but I always fell short in my own mind. I appeared confident, I was a "savvy" businesswoman, and from the outside I looked like I had it all. But it was never good enough for me.

Today I don't have the ideal in weight and shape—in fact, by weight, height, and shape, I fall more into the "average" American woman standards—yet I like myself so much better! Even though I am still a perfectionist by so many of my standards, I have learned to embrace myself and my imperfections each time I don't hit that "twelve out of a possible ten scale."

When Renee meets a woman in the department store, she is in total admiration. She asks, "What's it like to be undeniably pretty?" The total irony is that this woman is loaded down with all her own insecurities, absolutely does not believe that this comment applies to her, and scoffs in a disregarding manner.

The next day, Renee is granted her wish of being "undeniably pretty" in her own mind when she hits her head in spinning class. When she comes to, she sees herself as if in the eyes of an admirer. From this point forward the movie becomes, for the most part, a delightful message of self-love. Then suddenly the magic starts: Renee starts expecting others to treat her respectfully. She takes a bold leap and applies for the receptionist job at her posh corporate headquarters. She gets the job using her newfound bold, confident style.

When we come to midlife it's time to put the frivolities and perhaps grandiose expectations of early life away. It's time to look around at the realities of what truly matters in life. It doesn't mean we necessarily lower our standards, but simply prioritize the things in our lives that bring us the most joy. If your dream at midlife is to be the best version of yourself physically and emotionally, and live your best life, I say, "So be it, and rock on!"

Like everything else in life at this time, however, we need to embrace the journey and not only be invested in results. Let's face it, life has always been precious, but it becomes more so at this time because we know there's less of it to waste. If we are going to make goals and go after the things that are most important, we need to love and embrace the whole process.

While Renee is enjoying this whirlwind of a new life, she starts to feel like it is all going to her head and she is abandoning some of the values and friendships she enjoyed as an "average" girl. She becomes unhappy and confused and feels like a fraud—Imposter syndrome! It is just around this time that she hits her head for a second time and loses all her amazing infatuation with herself. She learned that she is beautiful, confident, and capable just the way she is.

This movie makes me so happy; I am just saying yes, yes, yes! I love how she becomes nearly best friends with her boss Avery, one of the owners and the CEO of the cosmetics company. Her boss and coworkers find Renee's down-to-earth joyfulness refreshing and new, unlike so many other of the "glamorous" types they normally hire. The movie goes on with Renee meeting a wonderful new boyfriend and climbing up the corporate ladder very quickly.

It is a totally delightful feel-good movie, in my opinion. Amy Schumer was criticized for this movie because the critics said that she wasn't "big enough" to play this role. My take is that was one of best parts of the movie: as women, we all share insecurities and a common bond in them—it doesn't matter what our size, age, color, or sexuality is. The self-images that we have are completely no fault of our own and have happened as a result of the way that we are cultured. Besides, Amy Schumer is just about the size of the average woman today who tends to be closer to a size sixteen than a two, and why can't any woman feel like she is beautiful? This is absolutely imperative! It reminds me of something Oprah Winfrey once said about Dorothy with the red shoes in *The Wizard of Oz*. "She always had the power." She just didn't know it.

My feelings about growing older sometimes feel like they have to do with my own biases, perceptions, and views on how I have always seen/judged older people. I remember how I thought about older women when I was a "younger." Some of them I completely admired and wanted to be like, while others I overlooked. I believe some of my greatest fears stem from my views and feelings not only about older women but also older people. In many ways I truly did see some of them as having passed their "time." When I think about this now, I have a great deal of shame for looking at elders this way. I also realize that is truly not the reality of the way it is or needs to be.

The amazing lessons from the movie *I Feel Pretty* are all the things we should be telling ourselves no matter what we look like, our age, race, sexuality, and a million other combinations.

When we speak about women that are middle-aged and beyond, it seems that most of us were taught to never love ourselves. Most of us were taught that was selfish and wrong, and our lives should be dedicated to giving and serving others. We grew up being told that it was our duty to put others' needs before ours. What our mothers didn't realize (and their mothers before them) was that how a woman feels about herself affects every aspect of her life, especially her ability to give to others. There is nothing wrong with a life of serving as long as we are aware that we need to give to ourselves as well. We cannot pour from an empty cup.

One of the great lessons from this movie is "Change your mind, change your life." Of course Renee didn't realize that this "new person" she became was all in her mind, but the final outcome was she learned that this person was who she really is if she would just give herself the opportunity to be confident and possess some self-love. What if we could change how we feel about ageing, or any negative stereotypes that we have internalized, by training ourselves to look at life and the world from a more positive perspective?

As a teenager I suffered from a debilitating depression. When I speak of this time I am remembering a self-loathing that I had never experienced before or ever since. I did not want to interface with anyone, and I felt a strong need to hide, even from my family and friends. Thank God I was not suicidal, but at that time I doubted my life would ever be worth living again. Recently my husband asked me how I knew when the depression and the "demons" inside my head were finally gone. I said that I woke up one day and my head felt totally clear. The only thing I had to deal with was a headache. That hadn't been the case in a number of years, or actually maybe even ever before.

I am not even going to exaggerate and say that positivethinking is what changed that—it was not. It took immense therapeutic measures, great support, and medical treatment to change. However, once I found my equilibrium, like an athlete in training, I read about and exercised the power of positivethinking at each turn ever since. No matter what has happened in my life since—and like so many of us, I have experienced much hardship—I have never returned to that dark place again. I know that I will always be fineas long as I continue treating myself with the kindness, care, and understanding that I would to any loved one.

One of my favorite singers speaks about how heartache brings more tenderness. She is absolutely right when she says that love can see you through—love from and for the Creator, family, friends, and sometimes even complete strangers. But most of all it's the love that we give to ourselves that truly heals us. I'll never forget a time twenty years ago when I was very sick, and I had been pushing myself so hard trying to power through. Someone said to me, "The world will start treating you much kinder when you begin to treat yourself with more kindness."

We need to take the time to allow ourselves to heal from past wounds. Sometimes it's hard to give this time to ourselves. As women we always feel that our priorities lie in giving and helping others; we may feel that we need to take care of others first and then we will get to ourselves. The problem is that our time never seems to come, and we wind up exhausted and depleted.

Am I always a great role model of this for myself? People who don't know me well and view me from the outside would beg to differ. At times I appear to have what many people would view as an exhausting schedule. This is true, at times I absolutely do, but those who know me well know that I make the time in my life for loving relationships, for my family, close friends, at least seven hours sleep a night, and several hours a week just to do things for myself that I truly enjoy.

Following my passions and making a serious dent in my bucket list are the biggest benefits I have been giving myself for the past ten years or so. At this stage in life, it's a bit easier because my children are grown and my husband is busy with and enjoying his work as well. However, he and I make time every day to have coffee together in the morning, at least an hour before we start our day; and most nights my husband, my son, and I sit down for dinner and talk about our day and anything else that comes up. I really have to say that nowadays, unless it has something to do with my immediate family, there are very few things that I will do strictly out of obligation. Most of the things I do are because I want to, although there are always some exceptions. To be here now, at this place and at this time, I am truly grateful.

While I have always taken the time for my family and have carved out time each day for them for quite a few years, I would "push" myself to keep doing more and take on more without worrying about the physical and mental health repercussions. I learned to do this when I was very young, working full time and going to school full time to earn my undergraduate degree. At the time I remember saying to myself, "I'll give up these three years in order to achieve my goal." I remember for those three years I don't think I had even one day a week off. Everyday of the week was a grind, but I kept saying to myself, "I'll rest later."

When my kids were young, I certainly did rearrange my schedule to spend time with them and my husband. As soon as my youngest was about seven years old, however, I began going back to school and working a much more demanding schedule, and haven't stopped since.

Over the last ten years, at various points, I was working full time (in a management role), teaching part time, and was also a graduate student. The difference today is that I am in charge of my own schedule. I make my own rules as far as how often I am going to work, when, and how I will manage my time. I am freelance so for much of what I do, I decide who I will work with/for and the time I will devote to it. I still work incredibly hard sometimes, but when I schedule my time properly I can take a nap in the middle of my day if I want to. Nobody that I work for knows and, frankly, they do not care as long as the work gets done. I am also very proud of the fact that this year my husband and I took our kids on a vacation that lasted nearly two weeks. We have never done that before in our entire marriage.

My wish for you is that you create the space and time to at least live part of your life for you, the way you want to. I am not advocating selfishness but when you are truly able to live the life of your choice I promise you will have more joy and passion that you will want to share with others.

I recently had the pleasure and honor of interviewing an amazing woman, Catherine Grace O'Connell. Catherine is the founder and CEO of Forever Fierce Media, a female-focused, message-based digital media agency. I was introduced to Catherine digitally when I found and joined "The Forever

Fierce Revolution," a global Facebook Community dedicated to supporting and celebrating the modern midlife woman.

Catherine is not only beautiful on the outside but also very generous and kind. When you look at Catherine you see the kind of woman we would all aspire to. She is a fashion model and is blonde, blue-eyed, tall, thin, and statuesque. She is the picture of health and vibrancy. By looking at Catherine no one would realize the kind of pain, both physically and emotionally, that she has been through.

Five years ago, Catherine was in a very different situation. She was suffering from late-stage Lyme disease and meningitis and her physical symptoms were exacerbated from years of trauma and abuse. Much of her pain and emotional anguish was healed by Eastern medical treatments and techniques. Finally, change began to take place; she says her life and spirit went from a woman who had no self-esteem, no passion, and an overall feeling that she had no future to a woman with new beliefs about herself that enabled her to transform her life. "I finally let go of who I was told to be to become the women I have always desired to be." Today, in addition to a spiritual journey that has spanned over twenty-five years, Catherine says that she understands that true transformation happens from within. Additionally, she says she has created and found her tribe and voice and has no inhibitions in using it.

Catherine has an e-book full of wisdom called *My 7 Powerful Tips for Finding Your Confidence at Midlife.* I would like to discuss and contemplate a few of her sage and invaluable thoughts.

Catherine says "Strike a pose," which means hold yourself in a way to show your confidence. It also means, for example, to look people in the eye when you speak to them, offer a firm handshake, and use hand gestures when speaking. As an instructor and coach that spends much time teaching students how to communicate and express themselves effectively, I know this to be truly effective in communicating because effective communication is only 7 percent of what we say. The rest is body language, tone, inflection, speech, and volume. Therefore when Catherine says to "Strike a pose," it is not only helpful for others to witness us in our power but more importantly when we stand tall and proud we feel taller and prouder.

Another tip from Catherine is "Tell yourself a new story." We need to fill our own "tanks," so to speak, with the richest and purest fuel to spark our energy and motivation that we can. If you are telling yourself harmful stories about yourself, by all means change the inner dialogue! Catherine says, "Tell yourself a story about the woman you have always desired to beand be her now." She also says if you believe you are confident you will be.

Finally, another one of my favorites is "Let your shield down." There is so much buzz these days about vulnerability, for very good reason. Part of loving ourselves is accepting and embracing who we are, warts and all. Once we have done this we have an easier time saying "I'm wrong" or "I'm sorry" and still accept the fact that we are human and we will make mistakes.

Today one of the great things that is changing in business is our ability to show ourselves as human beings. I have fully embraced this and taken more to business social media as Colette the person, not Colette-with-the-stiff-upper-lip "professional." A great quote from Catherine is "When we build walls around our hearts, walls that are no longer necessary to protect us, we keep people away (O'Connell 2019)."

Sheri Salata, who was formerly the producer and writer for *The Oprah Winfrey Show* and has worked with Oprah for over twenty years, has written an empowering book called *The Beautiful No*. Sheri talks about how the stories we tell ourselves are the most impactful and potentially the most damaging. She says that the stories we tell ourselves are the difference between the "joyride" and the "hard road."

Sheri concurs in her book that somehow we think of it as being vain or too self-absorbed to tend to ourselves and our own stories properly. To give ourselves the credit, kudos, and words of encouragement that make us feel worthwhile and valid is something we just don't do most of the time. Instead, we let our inner demons and negativity get the best of us. Sheri makes an extremely valid point when she says you can read every book, go to every seminar, sign up for every retreat, but in the end you will have to be the one to rewrite the stories of your life.

In the end she says, "You will need to be the one who dissolves the lies of unworthiness, not-good-enough-ness, I can only have this-ness, other people are luckier, things will never work-out-ness and recast it all with new beliefs full of love, beauty, grace, power, and abundance."

Sheri makes so many great points in her book it's hard to choose which points to discuss here. But there is a final point on how what we feel about ourselves shows in our physical state of being that is so poignant I feel compelled to repeat it: "Fifty-six. When I say it out loud, it sounds older than I picture myself in my mind. A lot older. And it looks different on everyone, I notice. I'm not talking about gray hairs or wrinkles. When I glance around at women in my age range, I can see so clearly how we are each telling such different stories about what's possible for ourselves.

You can tell by the way we move, by the way we talk, and the language we use; you can tell by the way we dress. You can tell by our energy, the smile in our eyes, or the listless exhausted stare of disappointment."

What does this mean? At this point in life, perhaps a time like no other, we draw and create the "picture" of who we are. My interpretation of these points is there are times we experience misfortune and have sickness and sorrow but we respond to these situations in our own personal way, and how we show up or continue to show up reflects how we "see" ourselves and how those around us ultimately will. I believe Sheri's points were so perfectly said and bring home the message of this work amazingly.

The tips covered in this chapter are hard-earned lessons that some of us are aware of. For those of us who are not, make these lessons and the gifts of self-acceptance and love your own today. Take time for yourself, speak kindly to and of yourself, and take some time to just be still, so you can quiet the chatter in your mind. You will not regret it—I promise.

CHAPTER 2

You've Come a Long Way, Baby!

———

The culture of our Western society, in many ways, has been difficult on ageing—particularly for women who are ageing. If we are going to change our mind-set we need to look at the visibility or invisibility that women experience as the result of our looks, particularly through social and mass-marketing media. Even if we keep our looks up throughout our lives there is no doubt, of course, we will show signs of ageing. As a woman, the idea of ageing in our society can be a major blow to our self-esteem and can occur when we are no longer being noticed by men and women. This can also be an incredible source of shame. It can become an instance of not only not being noticed for our looks but also being marginalized to the point where our "voice" can be invalidated.

Like any form of bias or discrimination—although essentially we are the victimized—we need to strengthen our resolve and find ways to internally (as well as externally) fight this battle. How do we fight this battle, exactly? We find new ways of looking at ourselves and other women, finding the beauty in ourselves and others. We need to train ourselves to stop thinking we should still look like we did in our twenties and thirties. Even though many of us can and should view ourselves as young, we have to stop scrutinizing and comparing ourselves to the way we looked, or wanted to look, at that time.

The other day I went to see my sister who is sixty-seven years old.She was so happy and bubbly, and that look on her was absolutely beautiful and I told her so! We need to be one another's cheerleaders. There is nothing I appreciate more than a compliment from a woman my age because I know it is sincere. I make it a habit when I see a woman out and about and she has something pretty on or I feel that she looks good, I will tell her!

My kids laugh at me because if I am out and a woman gives me a compliment, I will look around to see whom I can pass that compliment along to. Many times it is the woman who complimented me; if I find something that makes her look pretty (even if it is the smile on her face) I will say so. My kids laugh, and say, "Do you have to talk to everyone, Mom?"

Back in the 1970s there was a cigarette commercial/ad that depicted women having earned the right to "smoke like a man." The slogan was "You've Come a Long Way, Baby," appealing to the hard-fought independence of the women of that generation, or so it implied. In reality this was the tobacco industry's attempt to entice women of the generation to associate smoking with independence. Did it work? You bet.The campaign ran from 1968 well into the 1980s, and women smokers grew exponentially.

The image of the glamorous, independent, self-assured woman was the theme of the day in advertising. Although we look at advertising as a side note of sorts or by-product of the culture, many people, not just women, are influenced by its messages. I can recall a commercial about a perfume called Charlie, celebrating the feminist movement—depicting a young, elegant, and expensively dressed woman stepping out of a Rolls-Royce as her chauffer opens her door. Who can forget the Enjoli perfume commercial where the woman sings about bringing home the bacon, yet not letting him (her spouse) forget he's a man. There you have it, the media sums up the message of the day: women must be superwomen.

As a young woman, in my heart it wasn't enough for me to just finish high school (which I did through the GED at the same time as my class). I still had so much shame around it that I needed to "blow the doors" off it and go to college at a good school to make up for what I could have possibly done had I never left high school. In fact, my undergraduate degree was one of the most important achievements of my life.

I also had to be the most amazing wife, cook, employee, daughter, daughter-in-law, sister, friend, and eventually mother. As you have probably guessed by now, none of it was ever enough. I also dieted and worked out excessively in order to have the "perfect" body. I would like to say that I no longer have an obsession with perfection but that would not be entirely true. The good, bad, but great part of it is then along comes middle age, perimenopause, and my best friend menopause!

When I hit middle age my body would no longer allow me to practically starve myself for two days and lose five pounds.

I could no longer push myself to the point of exhaustion, skimp on my sleep, and manage on a few hours of sleep; my body just said, "No, you will not mistreat me any longer if you want me to cooperate. Remember that large pizza you and Mike (my husband) killed off every Friday night and then you starved yourself for two days to counteract the calories? Not going to happen anymore! Your blood pressure will go up, you will be bloated, retaining water, and—oh yes—you will gain weight." It was then that I realized if superwoman was ever attainable in the past, it's entirely a myth now!

Is there any wonder why women of our generation have had a hard time ageing? As soon as we hit forty, the show we starred in through the media gets taken off the air, never to be seen again. After forty, not only are we not celebrated any longer, but we also totally drop off the radar. How do we reconcile this happening when many of us will stay healthy enough to live past eighty? Is it any wonder we get depressed at the onset of middle age (around forty)?

It's fascinating to think about the way our mothers and even many of us (baby boomers, Gen Xers, and even some early millennials) were socialized and were told how to be single. Like everything else, the media—that is, mass media—had a major say about what our lives should be like. Some messages were positive, some were not at all. Looking at both sides we can get a good idea of where some of our images of "sexiness" and what we considered success came from.

Looking at some of the most prominent media of the day is *Cosmopolitan*. *Cosmopolitan* magazine came out at the very beginning of the so-called sexual revolution. It was thought to be very provocative yet liberating for young women coming of age at that time. Back in the 1960s the developer and eventual editor in chief of the magazine was a woman named Helen Gurley Brown. Brown was also well known for her highly controversial book called *Sex and the Single Girl*. According to Brown, the book was an unabashed self-help credo for the girl that doesn't have anything going for her; she's not pretty, didn't go to college, and may not have even had a decent family background (Dines & Humez 2003).

Through this book, Brown was able to catapult herself into a position of major power, influence, and prominence with America's younger, single, pink-collar women (clerical office positions). The book served as a "how to" extension for the single working woman and, most of all, as a way to "snag" the man of your dreams. Some of her notable quotes were:

"If you aren't 'overbooked' or 'overcommitted,' there's a very good chance you aren't getting half enough out of life or out of you."

—HELEN GURLEY BROWN

"As for not sleeping with the boss, why discriminate against him? It's like sleeping with anybody else; there are the good times, the bad times, and the affair probably won't go on forever, but the liaison doesn't necessarily affect the P and L— yours or the company's."

—HELEN GURLEY BROWN

"Do get credit *if you can—no use coming in on Saturday to straighten the files if no one ever knows you were* there."

—HELEN GURLEY BROWN

In 1965, Brown came to *Cosmopolitan* with her expansive possé of young readers waiting and eager for more nuggets of advice for single young women. Brown's main goal with the magazine was to have a guide for women to get through emotional, social, and business dilemmas and how to live a better life. Within a matter of a year, Brown increased sales of the magazine by a whopping 43 percent. By the mid-1970s the magazine had a following of two million readers (Dines & Humez 2003).

Why was this magazine such a strong representation of the coming of age for the baby boomer and Gen X generations? We will take a look, but one of the things I felt about the magazine (although I was never a regular subscriber) was that it was glamorous, cutting edge, sexy, urban, well informed, but a bit far-fetched. It was everything I was secretly curious about but felt I was too ordinary to live my life this way. I felt certainly the women in New York City or LA were enjoying lives like this (even though I live/d in Chicago). The magazine had headlines such as, "How to Keep Him Interested When He's Away from You," "Are You Sexually Mature?" "The Unfaithful Wife," "Be the Best Lover on the Block." For me, although I couldn't realistically expect to be as sexually permissive, the Cosmo Girl was always living an independent, glamorous, exotic, and exciting lifestyle.

Perhaps ours was the first generation of women that even thought about being single and having a job to support ourselves. Prior to our generation, the thought was grow up, find a man, raise a family, and live your life for your husband and children. There were also many of us that worked outside the home as a wife and mother to put food on the table. Additionally, there have always been single moms taking on full responsibility for working and raising their children. The dream never quite panned out the way we were told it would.

However, Dines and Humez in the book *Gender, Race, and Class in Media* have an interesting take on how culturally *Cosmopolitan* was represented in society. They claim that the magazine, at least in the early years, focused mostly on women who were considered "pink collar." This would include mainly secretaries and clerical jobs. Again, like all media, there seemed to be subliminal messages within the magazine that women had to buy certain products in order to be truly considered "The Cosmo Girl." In other words, if we wanted to live an exciting life, we had to "join the club" and purchase what all the other members were buying.

It seemed that the concept of Brown's Cosmo Girls was aimed at women without a college degree and not part of the bourgeois class. This magazine was meant to be a guide to social climbing preparation for the Cosmo Girl, to "learn how to be a rich girl" and play the game of the upper class (Dines and Humez 2003).

When I looked at the magazine back in the '70s and '80s it always seemed to me that the "stories" of the women in the magazine were told in such a way that not only did they have the best sex lives, but they also had the coolest jobs. Additionally, it seemed to me that one would not be able to have jobs like the ones depicted without a college degree. This led me down the huge rabbit hole of thinking that I was "missing" something because I did not have a "cool" job and the rest of the world had college educations. I remember looking at the wedding announcements in the *Chicago Tribune* Sunday paper and thinking, "Wow, I am really behind. I don't have any of these things; I must be a loser." Once again feeling that my nose was pressed up against the glass and that surely I was lacking! What I didn't realize was that I was reading the "society" pages. It would be well into the 1980s before I would even realize that our culture has various socioeconomic social statuses.

Although I have no regrets whatsoever about attaining my education, I eventually carried much shame due to what I saw as my rudimentary and "basic" background. In other words, I carried the shame until I achieved what I thought I should have had to begin with. Then, of course, when is enough, enough for me?

In my opinion, women should strive to be everything they want to be in life, not just model ourselves after who the media tells us we should be. Women should take the time to know who they are individually before they should follow a prescription of who someone else says they should be. However, the fact of the matter is young girls are very influenced by the media and many times are forming opinions of what the world is and who it is that they should be.

It seems to me that in the 1980s, when most of us at middle age now were either growing up or coming of age, there was a huge emphasis in American society on money, accumulation, and drastic self-expression, especially when it came to fashion and hair. When we look at pop culture during this time, I can remember the music: songs like "Material Girl," "Money for Nothing," and "I Wanna Be Rich." There were also sayings like, "Greed is good," from the movie *Wall Street*, or who can forget the bumper stickers, "He Who Dies with the Most Toys, Wins." There were also words for people, such as "Yuppie" (young urban professionals) or "DINKs" (double income, no kids couples), bringing attention to the status of wealth that young "college educated" people had.

However, what it seems *Cosmo* was doing at this time was encourageing superficiality, and this was all with the end game of "landing" a man. While I am certainly all about personal development and learning, it seemed *Cosmo*/Brown was all about the transition of "average" girls learning how to act wealthy—in essence, learning how to become someone else. The idea was also to encourage consumerism at its finest—keep those sponsors coming. This new and improved identity revolved around fashion and spending money. As a young woman coming of age in the 1970s and 1980s, I know I ate some of this up like ice cream, so to speak. To this day there is nothing that makes me feel better than buying a new lipstick or dress. I do also believe that it is normal and healthy to want to learn, grow, change, and move forward, but not to impress anyone other than yourself.

According to Brown, the very idea of "naturalness" that so many women embrace today was thought to be ordinary or—God forbid—average. In fact, circa 1966 an issue was called "The Beautiful Phony." The ideal aspirations of the Cosmo Girl at this time were to be white, heterosexual, and upper middle class. White working-class culture appeared more often but only as a reference point for makeover and improvement (Dines and Humez 2013).

In fact, the Cosmo Girl was considered a have-not and was offered advice and guidance as a method of changing their situation. Dines and Humez share in their book that Brown openly discussed the fact that she was a single girl from an impoverished background who made good for herself and talked about finally having her own version of the American Dream:

> "*We have two Mercedes-Benzes, one hundred acres of virgin forest near San Francisco, a Mediterranean house overlooking the Pacific, a full-time maid, and a good life. I am not beautiful or even pretty [...]I didn't go to college. My family was, and is, desperately poor, and I have always had to support them [...] But I don't think it's a miracle that I married my husband. I think I deserved him! For seventeen years I worked hard to become the kind of woman that might interest him.*"
>
> —HELEN GURLEY BROWN

While I don't see anything wrong with having been grateful to have a good spouse, I find it strange that Brown achieved so much in her own right, yet sums it up as merely snagging the man who made it all possible. For as independent and accomplished as Brown was, even she is acquiescing to the "norms" of the time. On the other hand, however, Brown represented something new and, dare I say, feminist when she told young women to budget, save money, and live on their own to be independent. Julia Felsenthal sums it up in her article for *Vogue* in 2016, "She was saying: Hold up! Don't get married at twenty. Date around; sleep around; put your career first. If you have a job as a secretary, become a lawyer, the head copywriter at your agency. Here's how to do it. Then find the man of your dreams."

One of the things about Helen Gurley was she was an expert on personal branding long before the term "personal branding" was ever spoken about. Another point that Julia Felsenthal brings up in her 2016 *Vogue* article is Brown's message was "You are the raw material, shape yourself, polish yourself, and go out there and get what you want." While Brown dispensed advice that could be considered denigrating and overly materialistic in some ways—which was definitely a sign of the times—there was no denying that much of her work was sincere in serving as a guide to overcoming gender class barriers.

It's hard to imagine that the ideas introduced by Brown through *Cosmopolitan* in the 1960s were not being subversive for the day and time.

It's hard not to imagine how Brown and *Cosmo* would not have been considered subversive as things are so different now, even though many of us still feel we have much work to do. The main job for a woman who wished to travel was that of a stewardess. These women were paid low wages, no benefits, and no pensions. It was understood that they were only going to be temporary workers. This was because as soon as they married they would no longer be able to stay employed as a flight attendant. Nevertheless, women were flocking to these jobs as a way to "see the world" before they settled down and married, which was usually an average of eighteen months in the position. In her book *When Everything Changed*, Gail Collins shared that in 1960 women accounted for 6 percent of American doctors, 3 percent of lawyers, and less than 1 percent of engineers. Needless to say, women were not expected to have a life outside of marriage and family.

As for me, I married at twenty in 1984. However, we did not begin to have children for eleven years; additionally, I did get to do quite a bit of travel for my job nationally. I worked as a regional sales manager for Cargill and was considered a rarity in management even for the size of the company. I was in the protein division (meat and poultry), and there were no other female salespeople on the team when I started. I also very clearly remember keeping my pregnancy a secret for a while as I was just being promoted at the beginning of my pregnancy. Nevertheless, this work was in the early part of my marriage, and when I did have my children, I gave up this job. It was an extremely difficult decision, albeit one that I have never regretted. While I have always been a working mom, I chose jobs that were more conducive to being a mom. By the time my kids grew up I had the realization that WOW, I truly have always been a part of a unit. In other words, every decision I have made in my life was determined and made as my being a part of a unit; first my husband, and then my kids as well.

Gail Collins's book *When Everything Changed* also references a woman she interviewed in the 1960s. This writer named Jane O'Reilly shared with Collins that she had never done many of the things that so many of us now take for granted.

She never received a paycheck, traveled solo, or been the major decision maker for any household matters.

Although I have literally worked all my life and made as much money, or even more a few times, than my husband, I believe that I never looked at myself as a singular being until my children grew up.

In the early 1960s a freelance writer named Betty Friedanof the famed book *The Feminine Mystique* talks about travelling from New York to Boston to interview someone, and how she stopped into the Ritz-Carlton for a drink at the bar. She said that the bartender said to her that they do not serve women at the bar and took her to an out-of-the-way booth by the women's restroom where she was to drink her whiskey sour. Of course, Betty Friedan eventually sparked a movement that would keep any other women from being humiliated and relegated to having a drink away from the bar.

Another topic that the book speaks to is the relationship between boys and girls and how they were either to be "romantic" or nonexistent; the only "real" friends that girls could have were other girls. Therefore, to most girls, boys were such an anomaly that girls became obsessed with boys and dating. Boys seemed to be these mysterious and alien creatures that only served one important role in their lives. The essayist Jane O'Reilly recalled some years later that the absolutely unbreakable rule regarding members of the opposite sex was that a girl could never call a boy. This caused a great dilemma when the woman grew up and, working in the business world in a management or executive type role, became extremely reluctant to call a male business colleague to discuss something over lunch (Friedan 1963)!

When we think about our lives today as women, there are still plenty of dichotomies about what we "should" or "should not" do. I have some newly-divorced friends whose notions of how women should not make a "first" move toward a man or be the one to reach out or call a man are still foremost in their minds. I feel like women should do what feels natural and not worry about what is always appropriate. I have never been one, really, for living out many gender norms. In fact, my husband and I started dating in high school, and I'm fairly certain, as I recall, that I was the one to start paying attention and talking to him first. He eventually confided in me that he was so relieved that I did so because, even though he really wanted to date me, he might never have had the courage to approach me. Look what we would have been missing had I passed up that opportunity!

The way things are today are so different than how our generation started and what came before. It's not to say that we need to change ourselves entirely, such as wearing pink hair, having piercings in several locations on our bodies, or wearing "body art," and boldly going where no woman has gone before, or does it? Well, I'm sorry to be such a rebel, but I'm here to say that if the notion strikes, "Why not!" The point that I am trying to make is that in years past, as women, we were restricted by all the things we should do. However, it's a new day, and we should do the things we want to do not just because it is a new day but also because we are grown ass women now, and we reserve the rights to be who we are!

CHAPTER 3

How We Got Here

The purpose of this book will be to take a closer look at mid-life women, how they were cultured, and why this cultural socialization can make midlife and ageing a difficult adjustment for so many of us.

In order to understand why girls, and inevitably women, feel that they are less valuable, specifically at midlife, we need to look at not only our generation and our upbringing but the lives and cultural expectations that our mothers and grandmothers lived through as well. We need to look at societal expectations throughout the last several decades to see where the cultural norms began in order to reclaim our power as well as empower our young girls that will be women tomorrow.

Since many middle-aged women are what's known as Generation X (those born 1965–1980) and baby boomers (those born from 1944–1964), it can be fair to say that we grew up in the most liberating time for women in American history. More women than ever before were entering the workforce, the creation of the birth control pill, and the first generation of the feminism and women's movement all began in the 1960s. In fact, according to *The Huffington Post*, boomers in general have been known to be optimistic, exploratory, and high-achieving individuals. The boomers brought about and were a part of some of the most significant social changes in history, playing a role in the advancement of women's workplace rights and the so-called "sexual revolution (Raab 2015)."

Gen X, in their formative years, experiencing the latter part of what the baby boomers did, were also influenced by feminism, the birth control pill, and the extension of the rock and roll movement along with the pervasive drug culture. According to a report from Corporate Finance Institute, "They appreciate the value of independence and informality and are also technologically savvy, more educated than their parents and are a more flexible generation. Gen X is attributed to generating a balanced work-life trade-off and is also synonymous with a higher entrepreneurial tendency."

If we look at what it was like to be coming of age in the 1980s we will get an idea of how and why we evolved into the women we are now at midlife and beyond. In a video called *Making Sense of the 60s* we look at how girls were cultured; when they hit puberty the paramount concerns for girls were attracting boys. This generation of girls was concerned with what to wear and how to put herself together. Academics were lower on the list of priorities.While making friends and caring for others was also important, there was always the most pervasive thought of her future—and that was marriage and family.

Magazines in the day served as a guide for girls on how to be attractive inside and out. Preparing for college was a part of this but still mostly for meeting boys and socializing. The focus was also on inner beauty, caring for others, and being healthy. One's balanced diet was for the purpose of being healthy but also for maintaining attractiveness.

If we look at the history of our ancestors and what was believed in generations earlier, it is not hard to see why we can be so conflicted about roles and relationships in our current lives. Additionally, when it comes to men and women, these beliefs are equal opportunity offenders. Look at how boys are raised, and more specifically, how they were raised in decades past, the idea of whom a "man" is supposed to be can be a very tall order. For the most part, many boys had been raised to believe that a "real" man is always strong and never shows emotion. He doesn't act like a "sissy" or throw a ball like a "girl."

Mostly, the boys of our generation had been raised to never show vulnerability. They grew up with heroes like Batman and Superman and believed they should be invincible. Like girls, even though most boys growing up didn't feel that they could live up to that image, and certainly struggled even more as men, the final blow comes when they, too, start to feel "old." Suddenly feeling that he is not tough, strong, or virile sends many men into a feeling of dread or doom. Hence, the myth of how the sports car and younger woman have been said to cause him to change his life while trying to prove he's still "got it."

When we think about how we can thrive in middle age and beyond today, once again, we need to look at how it has been perceived throughout the past, specifically for women. Many women like myself, who consider themselves a feminist or at least believe that women should have the same rights as men, have perhaps optimistically felt that women in the future could enjoy the satisfactions of having a career, family, and close connections that could be a part of a fulfilling life. Women and feminists like Betty Friedan in her book *The Fountain of Age*—published in 1993 when she was seventy-two years old—felt an optimism about ageing that was rare for women that age, even then.

At this point, for some of us, time becomes much more precious; our sense of clarity becomes sharper, and our sense of where our lives are heading can become a priority. That is, once we do the work to overcome the pervasive belief that we, or in fact our lives, are less valuable or viable at this stage.

For many women at midlife, we come to realize that we have been hiding a secret "me" we have been too afraid to let show even to ourselves, let alone the rest of the world. However, midlife is the time we can take to finally figure out for ourselves who we are and where we are going, and start to embrace this wise woman who has so many years of experience and learning behind her.

During this time and moving forward we also realize that there will be losses we will need to endure–loss of parents, friends, spouses, siblings, traditional job marketability, and perhaps health. But if we dig deep we can find that we are now equipped with the resiliency, fluidity, and ego structure to cope better than we ever have before.

CHAPTER 4

Both Sides Now

This book examines why so many of us at this stage of life will feel that awkwardness and discomfort that many of us experienced in adolescence, that we inevitably felt into our teens and adulthood when we felt for some reason or another we just didn't measure up. However, we are at a better stage now to more fully understand and embrace the little girl that still lives inside of us.

I was very insecure about my looks as a girl, and I always thought myself ugly. Much of this was because I was extremely underweight and received many nasty comments mostly from other girls about it. I also disliked my olive-colored skin. I was an outdoor kind of gal when I was young, so during the summer I would always be outside. My skin would get very brown, and while so many people complimented and mentioned my skin, I felt very awkward about it. The irony today is that I am certainly not underweight (although that kind of thin was unhealthy), and I am very happy with the color of my skin, especially when I am tanned. Once I got into my teens, however, I learned to embrace my "tanned" skin, and at this stage I have completely learned to embrace my olive and oily skin.

All I wanted when I was little was to be named "Suzie" or "Linda" and have the blonde hair and blue eyes. Then, almost no one had ever heard of the name "Colette!" I just wanted to be like everyone else around me. Back in the day, when I was growing up, everyone around me looked vanilla white (except for some of my Italian American girlfriends from the block). This is no surprise to anyone reading this book as these types of images were extremely pervasive in the American/Western culture. And while things are becoming more inclusive, which is a great step forward, we still have much work to do.

Although it is hard for me to believe today, there was a time for many, many years that I was severely underweight. Additionally, because of my depression as a teenager, I believe that more than a couple of my therapists and doctors felt that I had some sort of eating disorder.

I remember seeing a former neighbor when I was about thirty years old and had "filled out." She said that she knew my mother was a good mother, but if she didn't know that she would have thought my mother "starved me" when I was a child. By my teen years, however, I had a voracious appetite though I remained pencil thin. The fact of the matter was that I had a very fast metabolism and I simply, could not gain weight.

The interesting thing was that as a teen I was popular with boys and was told that I was very attractive because I had a good shape. The whole thing was, it never mattered to me what I was told about my attractiveness, I always held the idea that I was not attractive or not good enough because of the other girls' opinions of me in my grade school and early high school life. Even when I became popular with girls and had quite a few friends I had internalized the negative self image of my earlier years.

Female models have always been incredibly unrealistic in size. Most are a size zero or as "large" as possibly a size two. Considering the fact that the average woman today is a size sixteen, this is far from the women we see in our everyday lives. The research is overwhelming on the number of women, particularly very young women or girls that have developed eating disorders; it begins with a diet and some idealization of what the "perfect" girl looks like. *HealthyPlace* shared the following in an article titled "Eating Disorders" from 2017: "In a recent survey by *Teen People* magazine, 27 percent of the girls felt that the media pressures them to have a perfect body, and a poll conducted in 1996 by the international ad agency Saatchi and Saatchi found that ads made women fear being unattractive or old." It becomes obsessive when no matter how much weight is lost or what she looks like, in her mind she is never thin enough.

The *HealthyPlace* article goes on to say: "The average woman sees four hundred to six hundred advertisements per day, and by the time she is seventeen years old, she has received over 250,000 commercial messages through the media. Only 9 percent of commercials have a direct statement about beauty, but many more implicitly emphasize the importance of beauty—particularly those that target women and girls. One study of Saturday morning toy commercials found that 50 percent of commercials aimed at girls spoke about physical attractiveness, while none of the commercials aimed at boys referred to appearance."

The New York Times bestselling author Glennon Doyle speaks extensively about this in her book *Untamed*. While Glennon is speaking of her own experiences in the book, when she speaks of women feeling like they are in cages, she is clearly telling a story that so many of us can relate to. In the book she creates a comparison between women and a tamed cheetah in captivity. The story is about how this magnificent cheetah was raised in captivity, tamed to model a dog, and how it was subservient in direct contrast to the animal's true nature. She then compares this immense, beautiful, and powerful nature of the animal to the true nature of women.

Glennon can speak directly to the feeling of not truly succeeding in becoming "tamed" as a woman. At the age of ten she tried to squelch the parts of herself that she felt were too big and too much. She did this because she felt her feelings were too big, her body was too big, and she had too many doubts. Therefore, to not to feel the pain, she chose to numb herself with food and then force herself to vomit. This was the price she felt she had to pay to stay "small."

In 1994, Mary Pipher, PhD, wrote a book titled *Reviving Ophelia,* which has since become a classic and is taught in many women's studies classes. Dr. Pipher is a psychologist who wrote this book about the process of coming of age for adolescent girls of our time. The process and transition can be difficult and sometimes traumatic for many girls. Dr. Pipher argues that adolescent girls often lose themselves at this time because they feel the need to change into someone more "acceptable" and "attractive" to the culture surrounding them.

This is very true but in order to understand boomers and Generation Xers, we need to take a closer look at the generation of women that raised them. The boomers were most likely raised by the Silent Generation (World War II era) and most of the Gen Xers were raised by boomers. While both these generations were a part of and played a role in the women's movement, the pervasive thoughts within the culture, specifically for parents from the Silent Generation 1925–1945, were still typically conservative (CG-Generational Kinetics).

The Silent Generation believed, and for the most part, lived the belief that women were born and raised to be in a supporting role. Only some 9 percent of the women of the Silent Generation finished college—some went to college only until they met their spouse. The main idea for women of this generation was to raise a family and live a traditional life in support of her husband, children, and home.

While the idea of the feminist movement became stronger in the 1960s, women of the Silent Generation were mostly divided and some were still very biased toward a more conservative stance. This resulted in an eventual divide between women who opted to have a career and women who were full-time homemakers. Then came the 1970s and 1980s where the idea became to not only "have it all" but also "be it all;" hence, putting tremendous pressure on the younger generation and women coming of age.

If we look closely at Western society, we can see where the dichotomy lies: it certainly does not exist in a vacuum. Ingrid Johnston-Robledo and Joan C. Chrisler shared in their book *Woman's Embodied Self*: "In her classic study, Brumberg examined diaries written by American girls between 1830 and 1990, and she found self-improvement was a recurring theme. Girls in earlier times were focused on the internal; they wanted to improve the moral aspects of the self, especially those that demonstrated their femininity and religiosity."

Those girls wanted to be better people: more patient, kinder, gentler, and more loving, devoutly faithful and trustworthy. Around the midpoint of the twentieth century, however, self-improvement efforts changed and became focused on the external, on the body. These girls wanted to become more attractive people, prettier and thinner.Today girls want to be sexier as well. They have internalized the view that "what is beautiful is good (Dion, Berscheid, & Walster 1972, p. 285)."

In doing the research for this book, it is quite obvious that for women it is impossible to separate the idea of "self-image" from "body image."

"To men a man is but a mind. Who cares what face he carries or what form he wears? But woman's body is the woman."
—AMBROSE BIERCE

WOMAN'S EMBODIED SELF – AMERICAN PSYCHOLOGICAL ASSOCIATION

Beauty and fitness have become an indicator of socioeconomic class as well. Bourdieu (1984) reported "Members (women) of the higher socioeconomic class focus more on the body's appearance whereas those in the lower socioeconomic class focus more on its functionality. Those who can afford cosmetic surgery, personal trainers, and the latest fashions look younger, are thinner, and more closely approach the beauty ideal than those who cannot."

Additionally, Bourdieu describes how more affluent women can delay motherhood until a more convenient time by using infertility treatments, and they can afford cosmetic surgery after having children to maintain their desired body size and shape.

Like men, women realize that once they hit around forty, keeping a positive self/body image in our culture is not an easy thing. With the images from the media in mind, when women think of the ideal woman they think of someone young, in perfect shape, and the ideal image of success whether in her career or as a mother, wife, daughter, friend, or lover: she is "superwoman." Once a woman reaches middle age and she most likely doesn't view herself as the ideal, particularly in the eyes of the opposite sex, she sometimes no longer feels seen at all.

What does our culture celebrate? We seem to embrace very young, fertile, vivacious size two women. While we are starting to do a better job of embracing many body types today, thanks to the popularity of women like Jennifer Lopez, Christina Hendricks, and Kim Kardashian, we still have a long way to go.

One of the things apparent in media today is that there are not many women middle aged or beyond portrayed as main characters with a vibrant, active, exciting life, save for a few positive yet unrealistic Nancy Meyers films like *It's Complicated* and *Something's Gotta Give*. These movies are definitely positive and very feel good, and they portray the main woman character very positively. But according to the statistics page of the Women and Hollywood website, the sad fact of the matter is that in 2019 women only filled 38.8 percent of speaking roles among twenty-one to thirty-nine year olds. The findings were even direr for women forty years of age or older (25.4 percent).

What is bothersome is that even for those of us that still see ourselves as vibrant and vivacious, there are very few relatable characters in television and movies. The problem is that much of the outside world does not view us this way. This really discourages many of us from allowing ourselves to feel free and embrace this time that can be a wonderful experience for so many of us.

Aside from the annoying symptoms for some to debilitating conditions for others, menopause at this stage of life can bring out new liberation for some women. Since she is clearly beyond her childbearing years and in many cases her children are grown, a woman can experience a freedom she hasn't felt since before puberty.

For so many of us at this stage we find it difficult to embrace this newfound freedom. Many women are not sure that they even want it. The years of child-rearing and putting everyone else's needs before our own has left many of us with a sense of not really knowing who we are. What's more is many women will find themselves in marriages or relationships with a partner with whom they no longer feel connected or emotionally involved. This brings about not only a crisis but also a crossroads for some.

There are many women who struggle with their sense of identity at this time in life, and the reason for this is society leads women to think that they have no value outside of giving birth and raising children. While I believe that once you give birth there is no role more important than being a responsible mother, we must not forget to invest in ourselves. Additionally, while this role is of utmost importance, we need to remember to save a little something for ourselves. Otherwise these middle to later years of our lives will be a vague resignation of the present while still longing for the past.

In decades past, how women felt about midlife was never discussed or seemed like it was never even considered. We'd heard all about the sports car for men but no one had talked about how women felt, save the book by Betty Friedan in the 1950s called the *Feminine Mystique*.

Today, we realize that women have the same feelings of fear, inadequacy, and doubt at midlife as men. To be sure, for many of us, midlife involves reflecting on our lives, contemplating our choices, and lamenting where our lives are headed. This may even be the first time we have ever stopped to really think about the fact that our lives really are finite.

A big part of the problem or dilemma at this stage—such as the malaise, anxiety, or depression that sets in during perimenopause and beyond—is that we never measured up to society's "ideal" to begin with. There may also be changes in the roles that we have built our lives around—such as children, parents, or spouse—that may change or go away entirely. What's more is we feel perhaps we have already lived the best years of life, and at this time society gives some not-so-subtle hints that we have worn out our welcome and are running out of time, power, and perhaps the energy to adjust to the changes.

CHAPTER 5

Acculturalization in Girlhood/Young Adulthood & Cultural Beliefs/Body Image

---

Even though there have been many positive changes over the years for girls and women through empowerment and feminism, in many ways the world girls live in now is much more difficult and oppressive than generations past. With social media (online or digital advertisement) playing such a large role in the socialization of our girls along with the media (TV, radio, print), keeping a healthy and happy self-image is a very tall order for our children. The one thing that is evident in the research is that for girls even as young as in the third grade the most important thing is how they look. In fact, according to Dr. Meg Meeker—an M.D. who has spent more than thirty years as a pediatric and adolescent specialist and has counseled countless teens and parents—30 percent of third grade girls have considered going on a diet already. In the eyes of a young girl, being thin means being important, likable, and is significant as a method of getting the attention that she craves.

The problem with social media today is that everyone is painting a picture of "perfection" that is incredibly unhealthy for adults let alone young girls. When we look at social media platforms like Instagram and Snapchat, everyone is doing their best to show perfection in appearance. People look beautiful, happy, and are only shown at their very best. This can be a difficult illusion that can not only be impossible to live up to but very damaging to one's self and body image. So much of this pageantry, if you will, is no different than looking at waif thin models in magazines from years past. In some ways this is worse than advertisements because these are "real" people.

In 2015, a heartbreaking story of a young woman from the UK, Hannah Carpenter, killed herself after becoming obsessed with having a perfect celebrity body. In fact, since the year 2000—onset of internet and social media—suicide has increased 47.5 percent in people between ten to thirty-four years old. This young woman developed an eating disorder at age thirteen and struggled through that for a few years, but at the time she took her life her parents and friends thought that she had overcome it.

Her parents described her as beautiful, immensely talented, and brilliant. However, she could never see that. She was extremely sensitive about how she looked (her weight) and the clothes she wore. If any comment that she considered negative would be said about her clothing, she would immediately change. She also took thousands of pictures of her body (on her cell phone) and had harsh criticisms for all of them. She turned up missing, and the authorities found her body in a nearby wooded area. She was eighteen years old (Thornhill 2015).

Social media makes noticing how others look, celebrities or models, visible twenty-four hours a day. On a daily basis young girls are bombarded with messages that they are not enough. Dahlia Valle in her blog post about Killing Me Softly states "Pop culture delights in degrading and openly criticizing celebrities that have gained weight." She goes on to say, "When young girls look at models in advertisements they do not realize that these images are not real. Advertisement tells young girls and women that what's most important is how they look, and ads surround us with ideal feminine beauty. This flawlessness cannot be achieved because it is a look that has been created through airbrushing, cosmetics, and computer retouching."

Instead of striving to be strong, have good muscles, and strong legs, as Glennon Doyle discusses in her book *Untamed*, girls become "small" because they want to be less—smaller, unseen, unheard, and invisible. As Glennon discusses, this comes from a need to not live a "big" existence, that is, to be literally less visible, less heard, and hence, less powerful in order to be more acceptable to society.

According to a program called the Confidence Project that promotes healthy self-esteem and identity in young girls and boys, the self-esteem of a girl drops when she hits thirteen. All the natural talents and abilities that girls so fearlessly and effortlessly demonstrate around the age of ten become questionable to many young girls at thirteen. Healthy assertiveness and enthusiasm can appear as "bossy" to a girl this age. Why? Is it because she thinks she is bossy or is it more so that others tell her she is. Katty Kay and Claire Shipman, authors of *The Confidence Code for Girls,* share that by the age of fourteen boys' level of confidence is 27 percent higher than girls'. Girls start to experience pressure at this age; academics, looks, college, and bigger expectations.

Julia Malacoff shared in an article on Shape.com, "[Recently] many celebs are using social media as a platform to share their own body-image struggles as a way to both relate to their fans and fight back *against* these unrealistic standards. Case in point, Lady Gaga defended her 'belly fat' on Instagram. Chrissy Teigen explained she hasn't lost all of her 'baby weight'—and probably won't try to. Demi Lovato called out a journalist for suggesting her weight was the most newsworthy thing about her." These actions are imperative for celebrities to discuss because it shows their "humanness" like everyone else.

Make no mistake; the grandiose "professional" advertisements are still out there as well. About ten years ago a very important documentary on self and body image came out called *Miss Representation.* The documentary sheds light on the way gender is portrayed in the media today. The documentary states, "Girls are continually bombarded with unrealistic images of youth, beauty, and sexuality while their male counterparts are indoctrinated to achieve power and money with sexually subordinate sidekicks."

According to California Governor Newsom, images of women as less than, smaller, and limited through society's teaching tend to make women doubt their abilities. Newsom contends that it is women that doubt their own abilities and that of other women due to the acculturation of girls and women in our society (Acquaro & Siebel Newsom).

When girls grow up thinking that the main value of a woman is how sexy she looks or if she acts sexy she will have more value, it will be hard for her to seriously focus on much else. With the pervasive messages of the culture in girlhood teaching her she is only as valuable as she is sexy, she will be less apt to have confidence in herself or her abilities outside of the way that she looks. With this mind-set everything is performance, and she is constantly on display.

For many girls and inevitably women, our body is the enemy. Media conditions girls and women to feel that their bodies are never enough. We become obsessed with food and exercise; whether we are overdoing it or underdoing it, our bodies are always the problem. This can lead to low self-esteem and a lowered sense of confidence. All of this begins around puberty or even before.

It is true today more than ever, American culture is about the surface—obsessions such as diets, and even academics and achievements can become unhealthy if not kept in check. With our culture the way it is today, girls/women and boys/men need to ask ourselves what it is that drives these desires? What are the reasons for these desires; are they because we know what we want for ourselves, or are we doing it to impress others? I feel that we cannot judge others by what they want for themselves, and certainly our modern world gives examples of what its idea of perfection is and what we should want, so the big question is "When is enough, enough?" These are questions that I ask myself on a regular basis. However, I will tell you that I ask myself these questions so much less than I did when I was a very young woman.

I think to answer these questions we need to ask ourselves how well we differentiate ourselves from others—that is how much do we feel a need to be just like everyone else? I think, if there is one thing we can teach young girls today, it is to strive to discover who you are and embrace your individuality. Then, if you are influenced by society to pick up certain beliefs, ideals, values, and habits, so be it (quite honestly, who isn't influenced by their culture?). However, at least you will know that who you are and whom you are striving to become will be the product of your own desires and not because you necessarily need validation from others.

GENERATIONAL DIFFERENCES

To understand how we are raising our girls today, it is necessary to take a look at how we as women have been cultured, which can give us insight into why society, for the most part, is still influencing our girls that outer beauty and being acceptable or liked at all costs is more important than anything else.

Many of the women today that are approaching midlife are baby boomers or Generation Xers and are looking closer at how we were raised. However, the upbringing of our mothers that were either from the Silent Generation or the Greatest Generation of World War II can give us a clearer picture of where some of the difficulties have stemmed.

For girls raised in the 1950s the idea was to be feminine at all costs. Girls were not allowed to wear the same type of clothing as boys; they couldn't wear sneakers, and certainly could not play with the boys. Girls could not play sports, and were limited to playing house with other girls. Girls were also brought up to expect to be homemakers. They learned to cook, bake, and do housework. If girls were thinking of a career at all, it was limited to that of a teacher, nurse, stewardess, or secretary. However, the priority was to get married, have children, and become a homemaker.

From the 1960s on, young girls and boys began to have to deal with the pressures of whether to get involved with illegal drugs or not. Events within the culture like the Vietnam War, the hippies, the Civil Rights Movement, and rock and roll all started then and created a culture conducive to using illegal drugs. In my opinion, drug use became an attractive way of escaping the reality of the difficulties of this time.

In the 1970s and the 1980s, girls had to deal with the decision of whether to be themselves or adapt to the things that their peers were doing in order to "fit in." Since many were doing drugs openly, albeit an "underside" of the culture, the pressure was high to "join the club." In fact, drug use was so pervasive that the First Lady, Nancy Reagan, proposed a campaign against drug use, the so called "War on Drugs," and "Just Say No." In fact, on the urban scene, where I grew up, you were only cool if you used drugs. The culture, particularly during the 1980s, was to follow peers and not be anyone different or out of the ordinary, and if you were, there was a good chance that you would live a lonely or limited life as a teen.

In fact, for me and most of my friends I grew up with, the pressure to drink alcohol and do illegal drugs was a temptation we could not resist. In my early teens I tried drinking alcohol but to a much lesser extent than I smoked marijuana. My use of marijuana was actually considered the precursor to the major depression I experienced in my teens. I remember my doctor telling me that my condition was genetic but it was definitely exacerbated by my use of marijuana. She also told me that smoking marijuana was my way of self-medicating or attempting to take care of the symptoms I had already been experiencing. When I met Mike (my husband), we were both fifteen, we made a pact together to stop smoking and drinking altogether, and this is what we did. For me, however, the irreparable damage had already been done.

At this time (1980s), there was no doubt that being an individual was frowned upon. Additionally, much of the depression and poor self-image that many teens (girls and boys) felt was numbed by illegal drug use. In fact, according to the online articles from the website of Youth and Social Issues, starting in the 1980s youth perspective shifted from a more advanced-level thinking to a more shallow way of life. At this time the culture was beginning to place more emphasis on status and the way things "appear" than any kind of individuality or internal substance. These are attitudes and behaviors that have been a direct influence on the culture that young people are growing up in today.

THE ROLE OF WOMEN IN MARRIAGE AND MOTHERHOOD

It has been said that many from the Baby Boom generation growing up did not know the hardships and restrictions that those of the previous generations did. The baby boomers were born, raised, and came of age in a very prosperous time in America. There were more resources and opportunities perhaps during the 1950s and 1960s than ever before in history. Therefore, some of the complaints about this generation have been that they were not adept at taking personal responsibility in their lives. Baby boomers were thought to be rather inept when facing adversity and to be extremely self-absorbed. In fact, growing up in the 1960s and 1970s the message was "Do what you want to and with whom you want to do it with." However, at this same time the societal stabilities that they experienced as children were fading by the time boomers were coming of age.

Virginia Pelley shares in her article on Fatherly.com, "Between the years of 1960 to 1980, the crude divorce rate went from 2.2 to 5.2 which is an increase of 136 percent." Does this mean they are more prone to divorce? She goes on to say, "Boomers generally married young, which is one of the biggest contributors to divorce risk. Among twenty to forty-five year olds, the divorce rates from 2014–2016 was lower than the divorce rate among same age group in 2008–2010. Among those forty-five and older, the divorce rates are nearly identical at both points in time. Characteristics of millennial women who are married today, they have very different characteristics than those before." A larger question is how did the ideologies versus realities of marriage affect the outcomes of marriage and motherhood for baby boomer women?

In her book published in 1986 called *The Singular Generation* Wanda Urbanska speaks about how growing up young women and men were more attuned to the politics of sexism, the fear of potential nuclear devastation, natural resources in decline, and overall negative outcomes for the world being inhabited. According to Urbanska, these are only some of the many disillusions that extremely hampered the baby boomer's ability to trust. All the things that the previous generations depended upon for stability were no longer the same for the baby boomer generation; things such as marriage, children, and even religion could not be depended upon. With the divorce rate in the 1980s having climbed to 50 percent (50 percent of marriages ended in divorce), for many boomers marriage was felt to be a union of unreliability or semipermanence at best. Even for those of us that longed for the romance and "the white picket fence" of our parents' generation there were doubts about whether or not marriage was something that would last. For many women and men, the safer route, according to Urbanska, was to view ourselves from a "singular" perspective.

When we take a closer look at the way our generation was brought up to value the superficial, devalue our own worth because we didn't or don't have the perfect body, value only other's opinions instead of our own, and feel quite lonely and isolated within our relationships, it is no wonder this time of life feels so difficult. We have got to learn to show ourselves love and care and stop judging ourselves by the superwoman standards that we came of age with. We've got to "take a new picture" and value the woman we see right in front of us. After all, it is truly "her" opinion that matters most.

CHAPTER 6

Embrace the Changes...

———

It seemed to me that menopause was on its way forever, thanks to *The Oprah Winfrey Show* and Dr. Christiane Northrup. Christiane Northrup is a board-certified OB/GYN physician who empowers women to understand and take control of their body and health both physically and emotionally.

I started to spot the signs eight to ten years before menopause actually came (perimenopause). I think that learning about the symptoms and also the behavior of many of the women going through it on the show, I started to understand why I felt and behaved the way I did. And for maybe the first time, finding a sense of kinship with other women crossing this threshold.

Starting around my mid-forties I had a sense of nervousness and agitation about my life. I had more anxiety and I started to have some physical symptoms around that time, such as shaking very easily (especially in the morning). I remember one time I was at work, and I just started to shake, and my young colleague said to me, "Oh, you poor thing, my mother had that same symptom in her menopause." The thought of menopause and the thought of shaking made me feel weak.

I had this restlessness and wanted to make a major change in my life, but I couldn't put my finger on it. I was working, at the time, as a loan consultant for a mortgage company. And while I was doing well (Top ten in my region), it wasn't enough. Nothing was enough; I had this restlessness, yet at the same time a certain malaise.

After leaving my job in mortgages, I went to work as a Director of Marketing for a financial services company. This was short-lived, and I ended up finishing my master's degree in Organizational Leadership and headed into my job at Junior Achievement—which totally brought about the changes I had been looking for. Although this did not negate my physical symptoms and anxiety.

Some of the great things that Dr. Northrup brings to the table when it comes to discussions about menopause are some of the most upbeat and informative things that I have ever heard a doctor say. This "holistic" method of looking not only at menopause but the mind and body connection through health was and is groundbreaking.

Northrup shares that physically we can have difficult and negative symptoms, changes in the menstrual cycle, anxiety, depression, difficulty sleeping, bloating, low sex drive, progesterone declines, estrogen stays or grows (estrogen dominance), water retention, weight gain, declining testosterone, decreased sexual response, decreased sensitivity in erogenous zones, and decreased sense of well-being. Loss of estrogen (usually the last to happen) causes hot flashes, night sweats, vaginal dryness, urinary incontinence, UTIs, and increased susceptibility to vaginal infections. Is it any wonder that we all dread perimenopause and menopause?

This makes one wonder, "Okay, so just what is this good stuff and when is it coming?" The good news is that if you put the focus, maybe for the first time, on your overall health (mental and physical) you will experience a sense of health and well-being that you haven't experienced in many years, if ever. Dr. Northrup has some amazing quotes about savoring the moments of our lives:

"According to Chinese and ancient Ayurvedic medicine, at age sixty, women end their householder life and begin to develop their souls. Our fertility stops being about having children and starts being about what we create for ourselves that benefits us and the people around us."

—CHRISTIANE NORTHRUP, *GODDESSES NEVER AGE: THE SECRET PRESCRIPTION FOR RADIANCE, VITALITY, AND WELL-BEING*

"We are not proponents of long life. We are proponents of joyful life, and when you find yourself in joy, the longevity usually follows. We do not count the success of a life by its length; we count it by its joy.

—ABRAHAM

However, Dr. Northrup explains that this time can also be the greatest time for transformation since puberty. The difference is now we are much more emotionally equipped to handle our lives better. The thing that I have found is that perimenopause is looking at your life and mentally reviving your choices and thinking about the things that are not working, what you want, and how you will get there. While this can be an exciting time, it can also be somewhat scary, but remember the quote—"Courage begins at the end of your comfort zone!"

Northrop shares in her book *The Wisdom of Menopause* that according to a Gallup Survey from 1998 "more than half of American women between the ages of fifty and sixty-five felt happiest and most productive at this stage of life. Compared to when they were in their twenties, thirties, and forties, they felt their lives had improved in many ways, including family life, interests, friendships, and their relationship with their spouse or partner."

So true. Also you don't need to change your life immediately or drastically, just think about what you want and deserve, something you haven't done in a long time I'm sure. It's at this time we need to let our heart, not our head, start talking to us. Some of us may not want to take action (and that is okay) but we need to at least listen closely enough to hear our own small voice. Although the realities of midlife and menopause sometimes bring difficult realities to the forefront, whether we want to face them or not, once we get through the storm and take care of our bodies, health, and mind, life can be really good! This time of life reminds me of a great song (one of my all-time favorites) by Gloria Estefan, written about a time in her life when she had been involved in a bus accident that left her with a broken back. When she fully recovered she wrote and performed this song called "Always Tomorrow."

In recent years, especially since I found out my brother was sick, I have been thinking about wellness. Also, I recently found out just how worried my brother was about me and my health. He felt that my frenetic lifestyle was completely out of control. I later found out that my parents had the same concern.

Of course, my mom always made some kind of comment on the way I "lived my life" but I thought that was just her usual expression of disapproval; I had no idea how worried she really was. It wasn't that I felt that things were out of control, in fact, I felt I was handling things pretty well, although I was having thyroid issues. Otherwise I was pretty healthy and living my life the way I always had.

When I was in my twenties and so "busy" my mom would say, "Colette, you need to slow down, you are not a machine, and even machines break down." I wanted to say, "Who really wants to be satisfied anyway?" But I know she really couldn't have understood what I meant. Because my brother and I were first generation college graduates and were in the kind of careers that my parents knew very little about, I felt that my parents just didn't have a clue. How could I explain to my mom and dad the things that were important to me like climbing the "ladder of success" and striving to build something for me and the future of my family? How could I get my mom to embrace the life that I wanted when she could care less about climbing any ladders and having an amazing career? She had her amazing career with her home and family. My dad really couldn't embrace the direction that I was taking (perhaps he could understand more because he was out in the world working), and he once asked me, not out of maliciousness but truly not being able to identify what it was that I wanted, "Why are you getting all this education when you are just going to have babies?"

My brother's worries were more because he didn't want me to experience as much stress and mental fatigue as he had. I think he also felt responsible to some extent because along with my husband he was my biggest supporter of getting an education and building a career. However, both my brothers flipped out when I told them I was going to teach in China for three months; fortunately my husband was amazing and my sister was her incredibly supportive and positive self! Good thing my parents (God rest their souls) were not alive then or they would have hijacked the plane!

When my Mom passed (my dad had passed five years earlier) right before I went to China, and I found out my brother was most likely not going to recover from his cancer (when I was in China), I started to realize how precious life and loved ones are. I changed my life, to a large extent from the life I was living, to be more present to savor as much out of each day that I possibly could.

When I came back from China I could not find a full-time job. This put tremendous pressure on the relationship between me and my husband, but there is no doubt I was at a crossroads, even though I may not have recognized it as such then. I took a job teaching ESL to elementary students in China for a while, but I had to let it go because they were very strict about taking time off, and my brother was very sick and I needed to be there for him. He needed me to be there with him, and of course, there was no question that was what I was going to do.

I also set my sights on increasing my university classes (to teach) and building the nonprofit I had founded. It took quite a while to build the pipeline of contracted work that I now have, and like any other type of business I have built through the years it takes constant prospecting and tending to, but I really wouldn't have it any other way. They say that the unexamined life is not worth living, and I would agree. Just as I found my way, you can as well. You just need to have the courage to dig deep. My story does not have to be your story. However, I would encourage you to take time to reflect and truly ask yourself, first, who you are, and then what are some of the things you truly want for yourself?

I now no longer do things that are not in my heart to do. My work is a part of my life at home and revolves around the things that I need to be and do first, such as being a wife, mom, and human being. I feel like I am now carving out a new agenda, and hence, a new world for myself.

One of the books that helped me truly realize that life is not a sprint but a marathon to be run at the level and speed that works for me, as I am the only one I have to impress or possibly compete with, is the book *Thrive* by Arianna Huffington. Arianna talks about how she collapsed at her desk, broke her cheekbone, and got four stitches around her eye. When she found out that there was nothing physically wrong but this was exhaustion from the way she had been living her life, she started asking big questions from philosophers such as "What is a good life?" Women in stressful jobs, especially at midlife, need to take heed as they have a 40 percent greater risk of heart disease and a 60 percent risk of diabetes because we internalize stress differently. Arianna talked about her business, and especially about lack of sleep and how it can be so dangerous.

She also talks about how the most important measure of success in the Western world are power and money. The amount of busyness, lack of sleep, and essentially pushing ourselves to the limit is a way that our "masculine" oriented society measures success, and dare I say that this started with our generation! As businesspeople we feel that we need to be plugged in and on all the time; this has been the evidence that one is committed and dedicated.

This problem of pushing to the limit is something I struggle with the most. Part of it is that I always tell myself that "I need to do what I need to do to help take care of my family." I also struggle with the "never enough" syndrome that I perpetually struggled with when I "built business" for others. Now that thought of never enough when it comes to building the business for myself can still be difficult because what I do for myself is directly for my family as well. And after all nothing's too good for our family, right? Though I have gotten better, sometimes it's very hard for me to say no and create the boundaries that are so necessary.

Arianna also talks about how happiness is love and how we should be bringing joy back into our lives on a regular basis. She talks about bringing love into the workplace. Taking the time to talk to people, even people that you wouldn't normally talk to. Maintaining creativity in our lives brings love and joy. Giving is so important she says, "Giving is a shortcut to happiness." I couldn't agree more!

Arianna also specifically talks about how women will change the trajectory of this course and redefine success. She calls this time our third women's revolution—the first were the suffragettes; the second was Betty Friedan and Gloria Steinem. The reason that women will make this change is because women are paying a high price in a workforce that induces stress, sleep deprivation, and burnout.

Finally, Arianna talks about ways to bring ourselves to a more peaceful state such as happiness through the practice of "meditation." She says that it has been researched by UCLA that mindfulness and meditation helped lower feelings of loneliness in the elderly and contributed to less depression and a greater sense of well being among pregnant women and teens (Guardino, Schetter, Bower, Lu, Smalley 2013).

She quotes a great passage from Marcus Aurelius:

> *People look for retreats for themselves in the country, by the coast, or in the hills. There is nowhere that a person can find a more peaceful and trouble-free retreat than in his own mind...So Constantly give yourself this retreat. The second century CE Roman emperor Marcus Aurelius was also a Stoic philosopher, and his Meditations, which he wrote to and for himself, offers readers a unique opportunity to see how an ancient person (indeed an emperor) might try to live a Stoic life,*

according to which only virtue is good, only vice is bad,
and the things which we normally busy ourselves with
are all indifferent to our happiness (SEP 2017).

The movie and book *Eat, Pray, Love* had a great impact not only on me but also many women worldwide. It was strange to me because about the time that it came out, I had been having my own idea of wanderlust. While I had no notion to leave my marriage (unlike Liz in the movie), it was around this time that I wanted to travel to China. I knew I would be looking for a short-term teaching assignment, so my initial plan was to get certified as an ESL instructor (which I did) in order to teach at a summer school program for a month in China. However, I ended up not being able to go because they were experiencing an extreme strand of flu and were quarantining. Little did I know it would take me eleven years before I realized that goal, and when I finally did go, it wasn't to teach English but to teach undergraduate Organizational Behavior at HUEB University School of Business and Economics in Hebei Province, China. When I read *Eat, Pray, Love*, like so many other women, I felt a great sense of connection with Elizabeth Gilbert the author, and this poignant story of her life.

Though Liz wasn't at midlife, she was about thirty years old and at the crossroads that so many of us come to at one of those "certain" ages. For Liz it starts out where she is contemplating whether she wants to take the next step in her marriage, and that is having a child. She knows that she really doesn't want to and comes to the revelation after a prayerful night on the bathroom floor that she doesn't want to stay married either.

In this period of "awakening" Liz starts to think about all the ways her senses have been deadened, and she has no passion and joy for life. She realizes that since she was in her teens she has always been in and out of relationships. She realizes that she has never taken the time to get to know herself, who she is, what she wants, and that she doesn't know God.

The reason I bring all of this up is because Liz is now middle aged (she's one of us) and from the outside Liz had the "perfect" life at thirty. She had what we have all been told we want, at least many of us—the perfect home in the perfect suburb, and all the latest gadgets and toys that we are told by the media and marketers that we need.She wanted to fit the mold and the script until she realized that this was not for her. She came to the realization that she was dead inside and hated her life.

Liz gets divorced and takes a year-long sabbatical to Italy, India, and Bali (four months each) where she comes alive again and learns and relearns to eat, pray, and love. Although this is a totally drastic move and perhaps we don't want a divorce or we cannot or don't want to go on a one-year sabbatical, however, it is most definitely worth the effort to find ourselves again or maybe for the first time and give our lives a sense of passion, spirituality, and love as these are things we definitely should make a priority. The purpose of this movie is not to say we need to get a divorce, or that we even need to travel. It is that we need to be true to ourselves regardless of whether others think it is impractical or unrealistic. If we listen hard we will hear the voice of our hearts and spirit very clearly.

One of the things I would recommend starting with is to take some time for yourself, by yourself. Perhaps spend an hour a week to reflect on who you are, not just the person you are as a wife, mother, daughter, friend, or employee, but you. Spend this time to examine the direction of your life, and ask yourself how you can learn to understand and determine what your interests and needs are. They don't need to be drastic changes, but they can help you come to learn better what it is that brings your heart joy.

CHAPTER 7

Perceptions around Women and the Power of Mind-Set versus Age

———

From the moment Carrie met Natasha, Carrie began that oh so ingrained habit, that at one time or another most women do in this situation, and that is comparing themselves to another woman. It's that question every woman asks herself at a time like this, "What's wrong with me?" When Carrie looked at Natasha, she saw perfection—Natasha's shiny, long black hair, her long legs, and her classic and impeccable taste in clothing for the party. Meanwhile, Carrie looked at herself wearing this fun, sexy, cowgirl, albeit costume-like, outfit. Immediately, she felt totally out of place and inappropriate.

One of my favorite shows during my thirties was *Sex and the City*. This was pretty much the antithesis of my suburban, married with 2.5 children, and the white picket fence stereotypical life at that time. There was nothing more exciting for me than to watch these four thirty-something single gals with their amazing friendships, careers, and incredible fashion living in New York City. Additionally, of course, their ability to cavort with handsome, interesting, and eligible young men each week. It's not at all that I wasn't happy with my life, in fact much to the contrary. However, looking at someone's seemingly carefree and exciting life was a great place for me to escape to each week. Obviously many women felt that way about this show as it, to this day, has a cult-like following.

One of the best, a.k.a. my favorite, episodes of *Sex and the City* was the one called "Attack of the Five Foot Ten Woman." Carrie, the main character of the show, is madly in love with a man she calls "Mr. Big." Carrie decided to end the relationship when she realized he would not make a commitment to her. A few months later Carrie finds out that Big is now married to a much younger woman.

The truth of the matter is that Carrie knew about the engagement when she and Big met for lunch a month earlier. He let Carrie know that he was engaged. The woman that Big married was a twenty-five year old (ten years younger than Carrie) whom Carrie viewed as modelesque and stunningly beautiful. Carrie originally met Natasha (now Big's wife) with Big, unwittingly, a few months prior to their engagement at a summer barbeque in the Hamptons.

As all of us know, comparing ourselves to other women is almost always a losing battle. Most times we come up with some very brutal answers. Carrie spends the rest of the episode obsessing over Natasha. She spends too much money on a dress she buys for a charity function that Natasha is organizing, just so she can show up looking what she calls "effortlessly stunning." It turns out that Natasha got sick and didn't show up at all to the charity event. When Carrie arrived, and realized Natasha wasn't going to be there, she felt foolish and realized she shouldn't have done this.

The episode is so great because it speaks to women in a cultural language that, unfortunately, we all understand—self-criticism. Often we as women feel very inferior when it comes to experiencing the gaze of other women. What we don't understand, and our culture reinforces and profits from, is our misconception. The real truth is that it truly does not matter what anyone else thinks. Like the great quote says, "We have met the enemy and he/she is us." We are the enemy that tells us we are not enough. The larger problem is, personally and individually, as women many times we don't feel that we measure up.

This is the damage that has been done and it is where we, as women at midlife and beyond, need to do the most healing. We cannot truly love anyone if we are not capable of loving ourselves first. Once again, our generation is sometimes reluctant to show ourselves love because when we were being raised the culture said that we should never love ourselves. The difference between our generation and young people today is that they believe that self-love is the way to go. I say YES, we can learn a few things from our kids and grandchildren.

While the show *Sex and the City* made single life look glamorous and fun, the reality of what our culture told us (baby boomers, Gen Xers) was that a woman at the age of forty or more had more chances of being attacked by a terrorist than getting married (Garber 2016). Recently, while doing research for this book, I heard a TED Talk by Anne Phillippi. Phillippi is a journalist that has had the good fortune and great opportunity to write for such publications as *Vogue* and *GQ* to name a couple. There is no doubt she has had an amazing career as she is definitely "someone" in the Hollywood scene.

The name of her topic was "Why We Need to Disrupt Middle Age." She spoke of her milestone fortieth birthday bash that to most people would sound like the quintessential celebration filled with excitement and glamour. She described that at this most amazing party, where she treated friends at one of the most expensive restaurants in town, she felt nothing but emptiness. All the success and notoriety meant very little to her. She talked about what our culture tells us are alternatives for women that are not married with a family at this age are like. She says there are two–the cold business bitch or the crazy cat lady.

While certainly tongue-in-cheek, Phillippi is spot on when we think about what our culture tells us about women at this age. Women alone and without a family at the age of forty are often looked at as someone too set in her ways, only interested in her career, or a "man eater." Even on *Sex and the City* toward the end of the show, when the women were looking at forty, there was a strong need to have them paired up and settled down. Why is it that for men at forty they are hitting their prime, and if they haven't settled down, is it because they are ambitious and a great "catch" because they are financially established? For women, there is no such explanation, and for the most part, she is "left over" and undesirable (Phillipi 2018).

Something else that was discussed in her presentation was a book called *The Happiness Curve*. The author Jonathan Rauch speaks about happiness as a curve and that beginning around forty there is a certain discontent for men and women that comes from an estimation and comparison of ourselves to others, and that even though we may have a perfectly good life, we sometimes feel that our lives and even ourselves don't quite measure up.

The book seems to concur with the belief that there comes a time in life (particularly around forty) when we reflect on our lives, and it seems that no matter where we are in life or what we are doing, we seem to question (at best) our accomplishments and the value of our relationships. Hence, there are sometimes unrealistic comparisons to others that seem to express that the grass is greener on the other side. However, Rauch explains that somewhere around fifty we are on the upper end of the curve so to speak, and we are or become more grateful than dissatisfied.

A person that is very inspiring to me as a woman of "a certain age" that I believe has aged brilliantly is Jane Fonda. Fonda says, "The 60s are the beginning of the person's third act." She says, "Midlife is a rebirth," and that it is from this point that the human spirit evolves upward, to wholeness, authenticity, and rebirth. In fact, she says, it is the task of the third act is to help us with "finishing" ourselves (Fonda 2011).

It is through this life review that we gain new clarity and meaning to our lives. It is not the experiences that bring richness, but it's the reflection on these experiences that makes us wise. She so eloquently points out that experience, life, and wisdom make us younger. That is, it is these things that bring more peace, lightness, and "youth" to our lives, many times so much more so than we ever had when we were biologically younger. I love this because I have always believed this very same thing. It reminds me of a song by The Byrd's recorded in the 1960s called "My Back Pages" about being so much older when we were young but younger in spirit now.

In doing research for this book I found a TEDx Talk by Patricia Katz called "Light a Spark: Navigating the Mid-Life Malaise." She speaks about the impending sense of disappointment at middle age. It all stems from the memory of the question, "What do you want to be when you grow up?" When we are young, so many of us think we will do grand things, such as becoming an astronaut, a ballerina, an actor, etc. We find that most of the time, however, we leave those ideas behind to become more practical things: an accountant, a teacher, a nurse. When we look at the actuality of our lives at this point, they seem boring and unattractive. As we have discussed at midlife, we tend to, almost by nature and certain reconciliation, come to the conclusion that we have mostly fallen short. As Katz discusses, people sometimes make the decision to blow up relationships and careers to the effect of much collateral damage. Additionally, until we look at the value in our current lives, the changes we may choose to make could be drastic or even destructive.

She also talks about what needs to be done to give us more peace and satisfaction with our lives, when we do know better than to destroy our "sand castles" or everything we have built and worked for just because we may have fallen short on some of our expectations. "What if we have fallen short on most of our aspirations?" The answer to that question would be, "You still have the time to change some things in your life." Perhaps you take this time to incorporate some of the things you would like to be, do, or have. As long as there is life, there is hope. Hope for change, beauty, love, or growth. The major question is "How do you want to 'live' as you grow old?"

She also says if we don't take the route of destroying our sand castles, we find that what is there are the thoughts that we are missing novelty, variety, and creative expression. We need to seek and find out what we are curious about, and instead of asking about what we are now we ask, "How do you want to live as you grow old?" Said directly and plainly like this it feels like a sobering thought but nevertheless it is important to answer the question as so much about ageing is mind over matter. At some point, you should switch from the past and what you haven't done to what you want to do now.

A few years back, in my early fifties, I was beginning to feel really good like I was growing and had more contentment than before. So I decided to write an article (again for my community paper) about why fifty felt like the new and improved thirty. One thing that I must say is that what they say about the early to mid-forties was true for me—it was a bit of a roller coaster ride emotionally, but as I started rounding out to my late forties and early fifties, I felt a real positive shift in my psyche.

I felt happy, I had a beautiful family, and I had many friends and colleagues that I was enjoying. I felt attractive and vibrant, and while I certainly wasn't as thin as I had been when I was younger, I felt good about myself. I began to embrace my womanly "curves." It seemed the more confident I was in myself, the more others began to notice. Many times when I was out and about people I didn't even know would come up to me and tell me how well put together I was. When I was younger, and was more at my so called "perfect" weight, that never happened to me. This is probably because I truly was more self-conscious and less self-confident.

The one thing I learned in my fifties that I knew would be true for the rest of my life was that I realized joy and grief could exist at the same time in my world. When I was younger everything seemed so black and white. My parents getting sick and passing made me understand that even while they were more ill than they had been in years past, I was still happy to see them and they me, and those moments were the extent of my joy. All the while the grief that they were ill was still there, and the longing for the earlier years did not go away, but I was grateful to have this time. If I can take away any lesson from my fifties, I believe it will be that.

When I was creating articles for the local newspaper, I decided to write one asking the question "Is Fifty the New Thirty?" I had some great interviews with both women and men and got great enjoyment out of proving my theory that people were more innately content beyond the age of fifty. Some of the questions that I asked were, "How does it feel similar to the younger years, and what do you feel is better or worse about life at this stage?" Many of them answered that they were more carefree at this stage because for the women they could, maybe for the first time in many years, focus on themselves.

Many also said that they feel more confident, resilient, flexible, and happier. A woman named Diane said that "at fifty-nine she is in better physical shape than she was in her thirties." She said that "she was looking forward to making new friends, seeing new places, trying new types of food, wine, and travel." Finally, she said that "her physical health was of utmost priority in order to stay healthy and enjoy her later years." Diane was absolutely right, she did look beautiful—she had a spring in her step, a joyful heart, and a youthful exuberance that many thirty-year-olds just don't have. This light comes from knowing yourself, embracing who you are, and living life on your own terms.

While I loved having and raising my kids, I would have to say that one of the things that I am enjoying around this time is the freedom. The freedom to finally try some of the things that I always wanted to do like travelling and teaching in China. The ability to take a few more risks in my work and the opportunity to be more romantic in my relationship with my husband. There is a sense at this stage that as long as I/we have our health, we can (within reason) still be who we want to be! Damn the naysayers!

Another question that I asked to a woman named Molly was, "How happy are you being you, at this stage?" Molly was seventy-five and she said "she feels that this is a good time in her life as she is healthy, active, and social." To answer the questions of being happy to be her, she said "she doesn't focus as much on outer beauty as she does on being beautiful inside."

Sandy, a woman of sixty-seven years old, said that "she appreciates the hair styles, clothing, and shoes people over fifty are now free to wear compared to when her mother and grandmother were her age." She also said that "at this stage she takes more time and has more time to appreciate family, friends, freedom, and life in America."

One of the men whose name was Chuck, age sixty-nine, told me that "personally, he feels that age is just a number." He said that "he has not needed to change his life or what he can and cannot do, and he pretty much does what he wants. He said that "this time in his life is easier because as a younger man with a wife and children, he always struggled to make ends meet." He concluded that "his family is grown now so he no longer needs to have those same worries."

My final question for the people I interviewed was, "If your eighteen-year-old self could look at your life and how you've lived it, would he or she be pleased, or what would he or she say?" Carol, one of the women, said that "she would be proud of her achievements and who she has become as a parent." Marie said that "she is proud of the fact that she finished college and became a person she never thought she could be." Still another, Alice, said that "her younger self would be very pleased, she raised a good family, and she and her husband were good parents." She said that "she always had a positive attitude, then and now, and she always knew that she could get through the hard times." Finally, one of the men I interviewed, named Robert, said that "his eighteen-year-old would be pleased; he worked hard, took care of his family, he looked forward to his golden years, and now he is enjoying them."

It is uplifting to see how satisfying life can be over fifty. As we so often hear, "This is not your parents' fifty," we are seeing people over fifty living healthier, being more physically fit, and having time to enjoy family, friends, and life in general. Even though we are all aware of some of the hardships that can and might still come, we are equipped at this stage to make these transitions, and we have the resilience and flexibility to not only adjust but also build a new life as necessary. What's more is we can rely on our circle of loved ones to support us through the hardships and continue to build a sustainable community of peers and friends that share our values and mind-set about not merely surviving our later years but thriving.

The age of fifty seemed to come up very quickly in my life, and the idea of growing older sometimes scares me. But when I take the time to look up and look around, I see that all is as it should be. Though, as I have stated, I have always been aware, and I remind myself now to savor every possible moment that I can and always be on the lookout for the joyful moments.

CHAPTER 8

You Glow, Girl!

"I am not a victim, it is not my identity." These were the words of Auschwitz survivor and psychologist Dr. Edith Eger on Oprah's *Super Soul Sunday*. Dr. Eger wrote her first book at ninety. Today, at ninety-one, Dr. Eger teaches others how to turn their pain into a gift. People don't come to you, they are sent to you she says.

At sixteen the world Edith knew completely changed. Nazi soldiers invaded her home in Hungary. She, along with her sister Magda and parents, was sent to Auschwitz where her parents were immediately sent to the gas chamber. Edith has two sisters, but Clara was studying in Budapest when the Nazis invaded.

Edith married in 1949 to Béla, and shortly thereafter came to the United States where they raised three children. Through sheer determination and resilience, she earned a college degree, then a master's degree, and then a doctorate in psychology and became a world-renowned psychologist.

At ninety-one, Dr. Eger still counsels trauma survivors. One of the many amazing things Dr. Eger speaks about is how we have the ability to turn our suffering into a powerful tool. She believes we are capable of finding meaning in our suffering and become the person we never dreamed we could be.

While I am not comparing my pain to the pain of Dr. Eger's, her words do resonate with me. I, like everyone else, have experienced pain, hurt, and disappointment. There was a time in my teens that I was so despondent I wondered where God was. In fact, I remember a day when I was hospitalized that I asked him where he was. This still brings tears to my eyes because like Jeremiah 29:13 from the Bible says, "You will seek me and find me when you seek me with all your heart." I truly did. It didn't happen overnight, but with work on my part, and some unbelievably talented and dedicated mental health professionals, it happened.

My doctor no longer practices, but I used to see her twice a year for many years until she retired. She said my life is a miracle and I agreed. We spoke about how what happened to me was truly a gift. It was like Spirit intervened so I could get on the track that my life was truly supposed to be on.

All of us are capable of turning our pain into a gift that allows one to become the person that he or she was fated to become. On the one hand, when we go through our times of difficulty and sorrow, faith (whether in God or a higher power) gives us comfort and solace, and when we come out on the other side we find renewed strength, in many cases better than ever before. It is at this time we realize that we were saved. Once we feel this way we never look at our lives the same again. There is a renewed sense, or at least restored sense, of joy and wonder in everything, as if we are seeing everything with new eyes.

Dr. Eger looks at her experience in Auschwitz as one that helped her to find meaning and she discovered a person within that she never thought was there. Freedom to "enjoy the 'feast' of life." She encourages us to embrace the possible and not be a hostage or prisoner of the past. She wants to help to free the people that are in the concentration camps in their own mind of their own making. She encourages people to be curious about what is going to happen next.

One of the other things that Dr. Eger talks about is that in order to avoid "depressive" thoughts one needs to be "expressive." The best thing about Dr. Eger is that she doesn't and will not allow herself to think of herself as a victim. She speaks of looking for the good and focusing on positive outcomes. I can relate to this because whenever I try something new I always expect to win. The reason that I am good, even if I don't happen to win, is that I am always thinking of something new to try tomorrow. Dr. Eger said she felt that way in Auschwitz, and she always told herself that she would be leaving there someday. This is truly an astounding example of positive thinking. Another thing she says that I find absolutely remarkable is that she actually saw good in some of her captors. She speaks of the time one of her captors caught her stealing carrots from the garden and scared her with showing her his gun in order to keep her from trying that again. The next day he brought bread for her and said, "You must have been really hungry to steal those carrots." What an amazing person and example she is when, as she says, she looks at "finding the gift" in every situation.

The most wonderful things about looking at life this way is that as we look at our blessings and give gratitude we receive more—more light, more blessings, and greater joy. The greatest gift that can come out of difficulty, once we have gotten through the pain or grief, is the renewed joy and gratitude that we can feel when we come through our darkness. My Mom always said, "Hope springs eternal," meaning that where there is hope there is always optimism. This reminds me of the conversations I often have with my sister. She has not had an easy life; she has struggled with medical problems and financial difficulties, yet she is one of the most positive people that I know. Like me, she has worked hard all her life, and she is incredibly grateful for what she has. We both are appreciative that we are able to find the good in most situations, and we attribute it to the quality upbringing and values that we were raised with by our parents. We get a good laugh though when we talk about our mom. She was a good woman but she most definitely was a bit of a curmudgeon, and I think my sister Ann and I became so positive in order to counteract it!

None of us can change where we came from as Dr. Eger so eloquently expresses, and we cannot be concerned with the things that were out of our control. No matter what happens in our lives, particularly the unpleasant things, we tend to reflect and expect that our reflecting and ruminating on the bad can somehow solve something. It doesn't at all. In fact it keeps us from moving forward. If we let ourselves, we can just exist in a kind of time warp. Short term this can waste our time, and long term this can waste our lives.

I listen to Dr. Eger, and I am so very touched and humbled, like so many others. If this woman who survived the

Holocaust can see the beauty and embrace the joy, why can't I? Why can't we all? One thing that I have noticed about people who come through amazingly hard times in their lives is once they overcome it, or even sometimes while they are going through it, they possess a strength and resilience that can only come through faith. I witnessed this firsthand with my brother. I knew he had to be so afraid, but he always kept his faith, and he was truly at peace when his time came.

Another thing that is so amazing about Dr. Eger is that at the age of ninety-one she is still a practicing psychotherapist. She is one of quite a few people that I have researched that are in their later years and keep themselves "young" by being passionate, active, and living full lives. I couldn't believe when I heard Dr. Eger say, "I am much younger now that I am older," because that is exactly what I say about myself!

One of my major passions is fashion. Fortunately, I have a close girlfriend who is exactly the same in this respect. Her ethnic background is French American and mine is Italian American, so we always joke that we live for fashion and great food, many times simultaneously! Evelyne and I go to several fashion shows a year and are thrilled to attend and share this common interest. We also have a "stomping ground" that we enjoy visiting every couple of weeks. It is a lovely outdoor shopping mall in a very upscale area. Neither of us live right in the area (she lives closer than I do) but we both love getting dressed up, going to lunch, and then browsing all the stores. It is the kind of place where most people that go there are dressed well. It is "the place to go" to see happy, well-dressed people. I go there not because I am wealthy or want to pretend that I am, but I go there because the beauty of the shops and the people makes me feel beautiful too! I remember when my husband and I celebrated our thirtieth anniversary we went to Tuscany. Each night in the piazza was the same. People would be walking around on their way to dinner or somewhere and everyone would be dressed up. The people watching was amazing!

I have always loved dressing up. Today, people don't dress up in the same way they did in the past to work or otherwise. I am pretty old school though some people have referred to my style of dressing as eclectic or even eccentric. Fashion, in my opinion, is art, and I love to surround myself with the beauty of art as often as I can.

When we live healthily we are better equipped to see the beauty in life and make the most out of our days. Since physical health and emotional health go hand and hand, we have to pay attention to our lifestyle. That is what we think, how we bring joy into our lives, and what we put into our bodies for nutrition.

There is a great documentary that was recommended to me called *The Longevity Film*, by Kale Brock. He wanted to get some answers about what a successful and healthy long life looks like. He travelled to what are known as the Blue Zones: regions of the world where it is claimed a higher number than usual number of people live much longer than average.

His first trip was to Okinawa, Japan. He met a lady by the name of Yosliki, ninety-three years old. At ninety-three she still teaches art and sings karaoke. She didn't start eating beef, butter, or milk until she was sixty-three and now only has them once per week. Yosliki also advises, "Don't let your age dictate what you can do."

Kale also met Kiko who does yoga at ninety-one, and her best friend is an eight year old. One of the great things about her culture are their ideals on inclusivity. In fact, in their culture all interact and socialize together. Children are extremely important to the elders of this culture. Children keep their elders active and interactive. Kiko also expresses that people should keep their friendships on a lighthearted level. Additionally, she advises to keep in mind that food (the right and healthy ones) can regulate longevity genes.

Another Blue Zone, this one in the United States, is the city of Loma Linda, where the average life expectancy for men is eighty-nine and ninety-one years old for women. Each week in Loma Linda the community celebrates the Sabbath by having a day of rest, beginning Friday at sundown to sundown on Saturday. Smoking in the town of Loma Linda is not allowed at all. The order of the day is excellent support of one another as it is believed that poor relationships equal poorer genes and more inflammation.

A church named Crosswalk Church encourages activities outdoors, balance and wellness, and healthy wholeness. Many parishioners volunteer for the community at the local food pantry and cooking in the kitchen to serve the homeless. Another belief is that less stress helps with ageing gracefully and has everything to do with belief systems. I respect the community's belief in a higher power. Religion/spirituality simply lets one know where they fit in the world. Prayer and meditation are so important; slow down and be present in your life. There is a 50 percent decrease in heart disease for people that meditate regularly.

The next stop was Ikaria, Greece. This is also a Blue Zone island where they say that people forget to die. The average life expectancy age for a woman is ninety and is the same for a man. In Ikaria, life is all about simple pleasures and enjoying life. It does not matter the house that you live in, the car one drives, or the money made. Food is a wonderful pleasure, with eating a little bit of everything in moderation. Theirs is primarily a plant-based diet though. It is what they call "old school food," which means no processed or preserved foods. They believe in embracing activity, as they say that today hip replacement surgery can kill people over sixty-five. Every day one should move, walk, garden, and things like this. People on this island slow down and savor life—they remain present.

People in Ikaria believe that one needs to act young to be joyful and not let themselves age mentally. When you act young you are young. They suggest growing your own foods organically. Eat a little meat and plenty of vegetables. Slow down; find desirable outcomes which require slowing down. Find people who support you and those that you support as well.

The people of Ikaria try to exercise every day but not in the typical sense—more every day, less intense, more often. Enjoy a drink but don't get drunk. Just have more fun! Health and happiness are linked to community and belonging. It seems to me that these are very wise words of wisdom!

When we think of youthfulness and maintaining it through midlife and beyond, we know that there are many ways to improve our health and physicality. We can do this by having good relationships, keeping active, having fun, and acting young! Like so many people in the Blue Zones, we need to enrich our lives with a good healthy diet because beauty is an inside job!

In 2017, Bobbi Brown—entrepreneur and founder of the billion-dollar cosmetics brand of her same name—wrote an amazing book called *Beauty from the Inside Out*. It's a great book because she talks not only about the connection between eating healthy and beauty but she also goes into specifics about foods that are amazing for your skin. She states the reason is because they are so good for your body.

Bobbi also talks about a time in her younger years (like so many of us) when she was not aware and didn't think about the connection between her body and food. Like so many of us, Bobbi followed fad diets and found that losing weight by eating unhealthy foods did not make her feel well. She found that eating things like cookies, breads, and pastas made her feel sluggish and tired. She started to notice that she felt great when she started drinking water. She also felt better when she ate fruits that were not too sweet. The fresher and more simply prepared the produce the better her digestion. She began preparing her vegetables steamed and drizzled with good olive oil. She found that she had more energy, better focus, and her eyes were clearer.

Soon, Bobbi began ditching all the weight loss books, began to read about health and wellness, and started to focus on whole-body health. She began paying more attention to what goes into her body. Bobbi says that "health food is life food."

She learned from nutritionist Dr. Charles Passler the building blocks and nutrients needed for healthy tissue development—antioxidants such as vitamins A, C, E, selenium, and zinc. Dr. Passler said to choose foods that support digestive health. He also discusses the fact that hydration, sleep, and exercise are essential pieces of the puzzle. Sweating is a great way to keep pores clean and to be sure your circulation is optimized so that every cell gets the necessary support. Sleeping is when the majority of cellular healing and repair as well as detoxification occur.

Bobbi Brown shares a list of what she calls power foods—perfect foods to eat after working out that also give enormous health benefits. Her list includes bison (her favorite source of protein), salmon, black beans, cauliflower, blueberries, and matcha.

Like Bobbi Brown, I spent most of my adult life trying to lose weight and then maintain the loss. I have actually tracked my weight loss and gain from the age of thirty (actually twenty-eight to be exact) on through my forties and fifties. Each decade (between seven to ten years) I would lose weight only to gain it back and "then some." Then came my early fifties when my thyroid started to go crazy. I was trying to diet like I always had but all I could do was gain, gain, and gain.

Three years ago I went to China to teach and stayed there for three months. Needless to say, the food was very different from food in the United States. Though most of it tasted very good, there was a specific way of cooking with more vegetables and less meat or poultry. Another difference was I did much more cooking in my apartment than I was doing at home in the States. There was an open market not too far from campus and it sold fresh meat, poultry, vegetables, oils, rice, noodles, and fruits. Additionally, I made friends with four other professors visiting and teaching—two from the United States and two from South Africa. We all became great friends and spent quite a few meals together in one another's apartments cooking and eating together. It felt very *Eat, Pray, Love*. Also, because I didn't have a car I walked everywhere. In fact, there were very few cars on the campus. Most people either walked or rode bicycles.

The amount of walking I did in China was insane. To give an example, to walk from my apartment to the market and back in and of itself was ten thousand steps. That is the recommended number of steps for the day in the United States for a moderately active person. Also, in China buildings that are five floors or fewer do not have elevators. Therefore, that meant for me each day of the week (except for weekends) I would climb with landings ten flights of stairs up and ten flights down. By the time I came back from China I had lost thirteen pounds without even trying.

I also developed some amazing habits there that I brought back home with me. While I have always loved to cook and bake, in my everyday life at home I cooked maybe one night a week on the weekend. Because Mike and I were always so busy and we felt by the time we got dinner on the table, ate, and washed the dishes it would be bedtime for us and the kids. When I came back from China, however, my oldest, Ryan, who graduated college earlier that year, was living at home with us for a while—which we were all thrilled about—and I began cooking dinner every night. To put it lightly, the two years he stayed with us were full of family dinners with all the special foods both my kids enjoyed like pasta, Spanish paella, pizza, and baked chicken on the menu each night. We all looked forward to the dinners each night and it was such a wonderful time. While I have no regrets for all the "special" foods we ate, needless to say I gained my thirteen pounds back plus seven more! Ryan moved out last year, and while we are all still having great meals together, I have changed a few things....

Because I needed to get my weight back under control, yet again, I needed to find a good way to lose weight without changing these newfound great home cooked family meals together. I was talking to my sister-in-law, Veronica, and she told me about this great new diet called keto and how well it was working for her. To explain the diet, the full name is the ketogenic diet. The keto diet is a very low-carb, high-fat diet that has many similarities to the Atkins diet or just a low-carb diet.

It causes the body to turn fat into energy versus glucose/sugar. This diet (dramatically) reduces carb intake and replaces it with fat. This lack of carb and fat burning process is called ketosis. This also improves energy in the brain as it turns fat into ketones in the liver. This diet can reduce blood sugar and insulin levels, which aid in controlling menopausal spiked insulin that can become a problem. Rudy Mawer, MSc, shares in an in-depth article on Healthline.com, "This diet has also led to reductions in diastolic blood pressure and triglyceride levels."

Mawer goes on to explain, "Ketosis is a metabolic state in which your body uses fat for fuel instead of carbs. It occurs when you significantly reduce your consumption of carbohydrates, limiting your body's supply of glucose (sugar), which is the main source of energy for the cells. Following this diet is the best way to enter ketosis. Generally, this involves limiting carb consumption to around twenty to fifty grams per day, and filling up on fats, such as meat, fish, eggs, nuts, and healthy oils. It is also important to moderate your protein consumption. This is because protein can be converted into glucose if consumed in high amounts, which may slow down your transition into ketosis."

The one thing that I really don't do and never did (even when I wasn't on keto) was to consume meats with high fat content. In fact, for many years, most of my protein diet has been chicken, turkey, and fish—the problem for me has definitely been the carbs. I have increased my dairy consumption, particularly white cheeses (which I have always loved) which are many times my main source of protein for the day. So far this has not affected my cholesterol in a negative way. I was thrilled with the diet, and I never thought in a million years that I would have been able to give up bread, pasta, and rice but as soon as I did I noticed the bloating in my stomach went down dramatically and my knees stopped hurting. I was told by my doctor that this brought down the inflammation in my body.

It's now been a year and a half, and I have lost twenty-three pounds and it hasn't crept back. However, the keto diet or my version of it is now a lifestyle for me. I find that I really don't miss my old ways of eating. The great thing is that I am cooking at home now more than ever, and we are eating at home most nights of the week. Mike and Ian still have their carbs but I have replaced my starches with vegetables.

The only thing that I have had trouble staying away from are desserts. However, I only eat them a couple of times a week.

Although I am not advocating the keto diet for everyone, I have taken the time to do some research on this type of dieting and menopause. According to Dr. Mindy Pelz, the keto diet is helpful for women in menopause in many ways:

1. Better mental clarity—thanks to ketones fueling the brain.
2. Reversing insulin resistance—by increasing sensitivity to insulin.
3. Less hunger—due to consuming foods that are more filling.
4. More energy—because of stabilized blood sugar levels.

However, there are some words of caution about eating too few carbs in menopause due to hormonal fluctuations and loss of estrogen. To make estrogen one needs insulin. The estrogen is important in menopausal women to ease vaginal symptoms of menopause such as dryness, itching, burning, and discomfort with intercourse. Estrogen is also important to avoid bone loss or fractures.

Keto may or may not be right for you, and it is always best to check with your doctor before starting the diet. I can say that my doctor is definitely an advocate for the diet, and I have had my first year check-up since being on it, and I am happy to say that all my levels for my cholesterol and blood sugar (glucose) are better now than they have been in quite some time. My blood pressure is also so much lower that I am now taking half the dose of medication I was before. I don't know if some day I will get an immense craving for one of my old favorite carbs and get right back on the roller coaster, but I will say that I am planning on riding this wave for as long as I can!

Another thing that I have noticed, whenever I lose weight I have a new attitude about myself. For me, and I think for many of us, there is such a sense of accomplishment as I have literally done something for myself. I walk a bit taller and I sit up a bit straighter. And yes, the problem for most of us is that the weight sometimes comes back one way or another. That is always so disappointing, and I feel bad when that happens. While we know that extreme yo-yo weight fluctuations are not healthy at all, at this stage of life the up and down on the scale can feel out of our control.

If we go into our best health journey and we understand this, the downs (weight loss) are wonderful but the ups (weight gain) don't need to be that bad. In other words, if we can make it a habit to recognize the wins, no matter how small, perhaps we can look at "battling the bulge" as an ongoing challenge we give to ourselves. I am getting to the point where if I have gained weight I am quite certain that if I keep doing the things that I did to lose the weight, then at some point I know I will lose it again. I can say, the biggest upset for me when I gain weight is thinking that it will always be this way. It doesn't have to be. Remember, "Hope springs eternal."

Another thing to keep in mind is that we need to remember that a healthy lifestyle, happiness, and joyfulness create a healthy and lovely glow that comes from within. Nothing feels better than getting your proper rest, eating clean foods, and getting the exercise we know will keep us healthy.

CHAPTER 9

It's a Side Hustle World

Since I was twenty years old, I have always been in sales/ business development in one form or another. I started out in food distribution and manufacturing but left when I felt I needed a better work/life balance once I started my family. In the year 2002, I began my career in the mortgage business. I was a mortgage consultant for a portfolio lender. There was much to "teach" about these kinds of loans, and it was here I got the beginnings of my teaching/training experience.

One of the major things we talked about to brokers along with consumers was the need to be financially prepared in this way as the world of work was changing. We talked about how people can no longer expect to stay in jobs for thirty years and retire with a gold watch. We talked about how people today have to be their own "brand." I know that ironically I had no idea how quickly what I was preaching would come home to roost. Little did we really know that 2008 would officially kick off the beginning of the gig/side hustle economy.

It's no surprise when I talk about the world of work and how it has exponentially changed since the baby boomers, Gen

Xers, and even the millennials got started in the workforce. If we listen to the news or get on the internet, we are witnessing the effects of technology and the global economy everywhere. In fact, the new millennium brought with it technical and digital advances the likes of which the world really hasn't seen to this extent in centuries.

The digital world has changed our lives in ways that we never could have imagined. In this twenty-first century, we have found ways of doing business we could have only dreamed of in the past. Yet with these great advances, like everything else in life, they have brought pleasure and pain, good and bad. Every day, every month, every year we are advancing with technology at a pace that seems to resemble the speed of light! We call these advances in technology "disrupters" as they disrupt in ways that cause the business world to change in very abrupt ways.

In so many ways, business is more difficult these days than ever. Companies need to be watching the particular market or segment they are a part of constantly. The years of capturing and holding a pole position in business for many years is a thing of the past unless the company is capable of constant and consistent innovation or expansion (i.e., Apple, Microsoft, Google, Amazon). An example of such a company that eventually crumbled at the hands of their competition was Blockbuster Video; they were the leaders in the video/DVD rental industry from 1985–2010. Then came Netflix. Netflix started out with a less expensive and more convenient "in the mail" model of the business and "no late fees." Blockbuster was so caught off guard, coupled with inefficient operations, discord amongst upper management, as well as losing money for a number of years, that Netflix was the final blow. Therefore, for all those years Blockbuster was the "sleeping giant" putting their eggs in the wrong baskets when they should have been watching the little guys that were growing more powerful and threatening to destroy their business—of course hindsight is 20/20). When Blockbuster eventually filed bankruptcy in 2010, they had to let twenty-five thousand employees go (Unglesbee 2019 Retail Dive).

Between technology making business more efficient (creating less need for labor in so many ways), globalization bringing opportunity but at the same time meaning less work for US workers, and the real estate and mortgage businesses imploding in 2008, life as we knew it practically came to a screeching halt. I know this firsthand because I was working in the mortgage business when it crashed in 2008. This was not just for me but for seasoned professionals as well as young students coming out of college. I looked at 2008 as an opportunity to do something completely different. I left the business world, finished my master's in Organizational Leadership, and then went to work for a national and international educational firm making only a fraction of what I was making in the business world, but I truly wanted to venture into this work that I had always wanted to do. At this same time my husband's business was failing, and we fell on some very hard financial times. To supplement my income I also began part-time teaching at the university level.

In 2017, I abruptly left my Director of Operations position for the nonprofit organization I had worked at for nearly eight years. At first, I enjoyed the freedom to do some of the things that I had wanted to do for many years like teaching in China.

I also ventured into working in retail as I had never tried that and came away from that (very short-lived) experience with so much respect for the people that do this work every day as it is not easy at all. Eventually I tried getting back into similar work that I had done for most of my career: business development and business/nonprofit management. Early on, I found that jobs for people my age and level of experience were not only in short supply but also, for many that I had gotten an interview with, there was intense competition. In fact, for several jobs that I applied for I had five to six interviews and still did not get the job. I was shocked, as this was the first time in my career that I was not able to get the job/s that I wanted. My ego was definitely bruised! This was when I first realized that I needed to take a new "snapshot" of my own career and life. I decided I had to change my focus and first make sure I was bringing in some income (quickly), make a plan, and then work my plan.

One of the first things I decided to do was to start my own nonprofit called Education for Growth. The nonprofit consists of working with young people (kindergarten to college) and people with developmental disabilities, teaching workshops on empowerment, emotional intelligence, cultural diversity, and positive psychology. I got reacquainted with a corporate sponsor that I had developed and grown with the previous nonprofit I worked for and they were more than happy to support my new mission (as well keep working with my former employers).

After that I worked on increasing my course load with the colleges that I had already been teaching with and added some new ones. This included the university I taught on behalf of in China (there are campuses here in Chicago). While this sounds wonderful, and it is, it took me quite a while to build this up, and it has been very sporadic. I also got some very good advice from one of my contacts at the college that said instead of pursuing a DBA or PhD I should get an MBA because this will give me more leeway when applying to teach undergraduate courses. I felt that was good advice so I began an MBA program at one of the colleges where I was teaching.

I then finally followed up on my ESL training that I'd had some years back and began virtually teaching English to elementary students that were located in China. Over these last three and a half years, I have taken on as many side hustles (gigs) as I could to the point where they are now all synchronous and compatible with my talents and background. One of the many things that I learned from my years in business development is sometimes you just need to throw the spaghetti at the wall to see how much of it "sticks." Because like the "disrupters" with the big or smaller businesses, things are always changing, that is coming and going, starting and stopping, and one has to be fully prepared for the next loss or opportunity.

I have now begun to build myself up to the point where I am doing well enough that I don't need to work a full-time job and would never want to again! As some of my gigs come and go, I replace them with new ones. Over the last year and a half I have permanently added Career Coaching and workshops with an educational consulting firm here in the Chicago area (part-time), along with getting a real estate license (I have some good friends in real estate and will be partnering to sell homes), and eventually I plan on teaching real estate classes as well. Even though you may think my schedule is, or maybe I am, insane, the things that I am doing are manageable as they are only what I choose to do. I really don't think people could say that as much in the old economy. All I've done to create this situation for myself has simply been to put my job skills—business development, sales, and teaching—and job interviewing skills to work.

If you learn to be flexible and take a new "snapshot" of your own life you can create things that you never knew were possible. Having more clarity about who I am and my strengths and weaknesses has helped me tremendously in creating my work life today. Since I am mostly a contracted employee for the organizations that I work for, I must always be looking to develop new partnerships and opportunities as absolutely nothing is guaranteed. If I look at this from a creative perspective, this is not at all different than what I have done for others (companies) in business development. The difference now is I am doing this for myself!

Today, gigs and side hustles have become mainstream and many of them are no longer another side, they are now "center of the plate" so to speak. These once side hustles have turned into viable businesses. The good news for us is that women are now leading the charge in this arena.

Writer Maddie Shepherd shares a list on the Fundera website that details some amazing women-owned business statistics. Some of the most notable are that the United States alone has 12.3 million women-owned businesses and those businesses generate 1.8 trillion dollars a year. Women-owned businesses added half a million jobs between 1997 and 2007. And 62 percent of women entrepreneurs earn their primary income from their business.

To take a closer look at the gig economy and how it can be helpful to women, we only need to look at how, for many women, although they may have full-time jobs, are also involved in household responsibilities. Many opportunities that are involved in gig type work are very flexible, affording a balance between personal and professional life. This should not be overlooked as they are not simply "part-time" jobs but jobs where women find the best ways to use their skills, experience, and creative ideas (Lakhatia 2019).

Gigging is also helping women earn money for the things that they do well. The gig economy has created opportunities for women to continue upskilling capabilities and specialize in their respective fields as a constant exercise (Lakhotia 2019).

Today there are many projects and new businesses that a woman can do from the comfort of her home or from just about anywhere. This situation allows for more women than ever to not only work but also be able to do so from just about anywhere. For women of our generation these situations create opportunities to do this type of work long into retirement. In fact, it has been suggested that by the year 2030 nearly 80 percent of the workforce will be doing this kind of work.

Since I have talked about my own story and have given some information and statistics on what women are doing in the workforce, I wanted to interview some women entrepreneurs along with women who have made a significant impact and have served as the intrapreneurs of their respective organizations.

While there are some amazing opportunities that exist for women of our generation and I am so excited to tell the stories of some very successful entrepreneurs, I also want to share some of the difficulties of building a successful business or career at this stage as well. Nothing creates better resiliency and stamina than the gift of perceived failure from time to time. This is not a new situation for most entrepreneurs, and the way we deal with and raise ourselves up from what looks like failure is just a stepping-stone from where we've been and where we are now heading. I have always said wherever there is life, there is hope.

A very inspirational writer and professional woman who tells her story and the hardships she experienced but also talks about how she is building a new life now is Elizabeth White. One of the things that I love most about her book is she gives so many resources for how we can help ourselves as well. In her book 55, *Underemployed, and Faking Normal*, Elizabeth speaks about how she does not look like a person struggling to keep her electricity on as she has impeccable clothing—because her clothing still looks good from when she had a good income—yet she meets the eligibility requirements for food stamps. She says, "You know her." She's the once very successful woman with amazing academic credentials—master's degree in International Studies from John Hopkins University, an MBA from Harvard, and a Bachelor's in Political Science from Oberlin College.

Elizabeth had achieved success as an executive at the World Bank, CEO of a nonprofit, and cofounder of a chain of decorative home stores on the East Coast. She was not and is not the kind of woman that we expect to see "down and out" but it happened, and while her story is frightening to the rest of us, Elizabeth epitomizes some of the harsh realities for women our age.

In her book and TED talk Elizabeth tells the story of an immensely successful woman then and now, which gives pause to our very definition about the meaning of what success is in our culture. I so strongly recommend reading her book or viewing her TED talk as she is a lesson in resiliency and inspiration. What I also find amazing is that she addresses some of the issues in our economy and culture that baby boomers are the first to experience as they are of retirement age.

She talks about baby boomers being frivolous and wasteful too. In his article about Elizabeth White in *Forbes*, writer Richard Eisenberg shares: "White admits she has made some bad financial choices and concedes some of her fellow boomers who've run into difficulties did too. But, she says in the talk, 'Millions of boomer-age Americans did not land here because of too many trips to Starbucks.' What happened, she says, was: flat and falling wages, disappearing pensions and 'through-the-roof costs of housing, health care and education.'"

This does not include the added age discrimination when we turned a "certain" age.

These are the realities of our lives today, and young people starting out in the job market are in the same circumstances only they have an entire work life ahead of them. It seems to me that we are both in the same camp: limited traditional job availability and like us, they need to "Do the Hustle!" However, even though there is no doubt this is a more difficult work world, if we look at it constructively, we can find new avenues for success and help one another build a new economy. This new way of working and looking at work can possibly be better than any way it has been done before. We can become the masters of our own fate and the captains of our ships. Once we learn "how to fish" for ourselves we will not need to rely on huge corporations to take care of us.

For our generation who remember how we started out, we probably feel like this is a raw deal, and frankly, yes, it can feel that way. However, we also know that at this stage of life we need to learn to bend. There's a great classic country song that talks about an old oak tree that was never broken by the wind because it was strong enough to bend. This is how we now need to look at ourselves. We have lived long enough to experience some real hardships and in order to move forward in peace and balance, we need to try to "take a new picture" and get on with our lives.

This brings us to the amazing stories of some enterprising women that I am honored to share. My first story is from a woman who used the strength and character she developed from living a difficult young life. Dr. Sam Collins lost her mother to suicide as a very young adult. In her book *Radio Heaven*, Sam discusses how losing her mother made her realize that as women we take on so much and often don't ask for the support we need or even reach out to others in our darkest moments. Dr. Collins has made it her life's work to reach out to, be there for, and serve as a mentor, beacon, and example to literally millions of women all over the world as a dedication and in remembrance of her mother.

Dr. Collins has been named one of the "Top 200 Women to Impact Business and Industry" by her Majesty, the Queen of England. She is also an active campaigner on the role of business in solving world issues, supporting families after suicide, the worldwide orphan crisis, and empowering women as leaders in developing and emerging economies.

Recently I was fortunate enough to have an interview with Sam. One of the questions I asked was about, her leadership qualities. I asked her if she feels that she has always had leadership qualities as in her book it seemed that way, or if she feels that she more or less developed them. She said that she would like to say that she developed them but she feels that she always had leadership traits from the beginning. Her book was so inspiring as to how she worked her way up in her career to realize her dreams. Through her leadership and successes she would go on to found Aspire in 2001 and has spent the last twenty years building the life that she wanted—literally bringing along millions of other women to realize their own dreams and destiny.

Sam now lives in the Los Angeles area here in the United States with her husband, two young sons, and adopted daughter Grace from the Democratic Republic of Congo. Sam is living proof that having faith and believing in oneself allows one to accomplish their goals and be the magical light and inspiration to so many others.

Another friend and colleague of mine that I had the privilege of interviewing is Bethany Mead of CEANCI, Career Education Associates of North Central Illinois. Beth is the community outreach specialist for this government-funded agency that provides career and technical education programs for high school students. This program brings entrepreneurs together with high school students. One of the primary duties of Beth's position is to develop and grow these relationships.

When I think of Beth, the word "intrapreneur" comes to mind as she is not the founder of her organization but she operates as if she is. She is creative, innovative, and she is passionate about helping the students prep for future careers and connecting them with business partners. Beth feels that the biggest contribution she makes in her role is making students aware of career opportunities. "They don't know what they don't know," she says. Funding for this social enterprise mostly comes from the state with a federal funds match. Beth finds bringing students together with businesses and helping kids find their path along with finding value and purpose in their lives are the very best things about her role.

Beth was also kind enough to bring me together with three of the many entrepreneurs that participate in her program. My first interview was with Karen Arce. As an intrapreneur Karen is an independent marketing rep. The name of the company is Medicare 411.

Karen helps people find and enroll in Medicare insurance and helps them determine which program suits them best. Karen is certified as an insurance agent. Starting her business was very difficult, she says. Being married and not living beyond their means she was, however, able to weather the financial storm from the ground up. Karen continues to market her business through networking groups such as BMI: Business Marketing International.

Right now she is happy to say that her biggest challenge is that her services are in high demand (the majority of her business takes place in the fall). When I asked her the best thing about her work she said, "Helping others get the best coverage for their money," and "all the interesting people she meets." I asked what her biggest responsibility is and she said, "Getting it right and being accurate." I asked Karen how she managed starting and growing the business and she said, "It was very up and down the first few years, but I was fortunate enough to live on my husband's salary. But this called for truly cutting corners as much as we could and living on much less than we were used to. "

Another entrepreneur that owns a daycare called Stepping Stones is Toni Brown, and she has been in business for thirty years. Toni started in daycare work after she received her bachelor's degree in Elementary Education. She became the director of the preschool, but when she started, it was a small center owned by a husband and wife team. Eventually, the couple sold the daycare to Toni. However, when Toni bought the business she was also working for a construction company, and she stayed working this other job for another twelve years while owning the daycare. She hired someone to run the daycare and there were many days when she worked sixteen to eighteen hours.

Toni also took out a loan for $25,000 when she started the business that her dad cosigned for. She says that when she bought the business she bought it on "good faith," the only thing she had were fifty kids attending. Five years later she had a second center with thirty-two employees. She, like so many others, experienced financial downturn in 2008 when she had to lay off 50 percent of her staff. Currently with the COVID-19 virus she is experiencing financial hardships again, but she says she is more prepared now having gone through the previous difficulty (in 2008). When I asked her what she enjoyed the most about being in her own business, she said "working with the kids and the flexibility in her lifestyle."

Another wonderful entrepreneur that I had the pleasure of interviewing is Leila MacQueen. Leila is the president of the Circle of Wellness Organization. She studied management and marketing in college and is also a trained and licensed massage therapist. She started her business with a grant from the Small Business Administration. Working as an independent massage therapist, Leila worked from 9:00 a.m. to 9:00 p.m. Monday through Saturday in a 300 square foot office and borrowed $30,000 from her dad to get her business started. It took Leila four years to earn her own salary from the business and two years not taking income from her "separate" earnings to pay the business's bills. Leila also did very grassroots-type marketing using the telephone book and doing door to door flyers and signs. She says that she absolutely loves the marketing part of her work—no surprise, she is an absolute dynamo! I asked her what her most challenging thing about owning her business is and she said, "First, don't expect others to work as hard as you do," and "Managing employees and keeping work life balance." When I asked her what she enjoys most about having her business she said, "It is the success that is most important, not money." Leila is celebrating twenty years in business.

These stories are about women with great motivation and resilience to develop a business they can be proud of and call their own. As we grow older there is no time to let ourselves stand still. When we stand still, we stagnate, and when we stagnate, we deteriorate. We need to keep it moving! This doesn't mean we can never rest or let ourselves experience joy, quite the contrary—we need to give ourselves enough rest and experience joy to move forward in a positive and productive way. I realize that this can be quite contradictory from the lessons we internalized from our culture when we came of age. Remember the quotes, "He who dies with the most toys wins," and "Greed is good?" Today is a new day, and we need to leave a legacy of resilience, self-sufficiency, and community for our kids and all the generations to follow.

What is being required of us today, ironically quite parallel to young people, is we need to find ways to survive through unconventional methods. We need to kick into high gear that great work ethic that our generation was quite famous for and redirect it toward giving ourselves a sense of purpose and passion for more enriched, fulfilling, and secure lives.

CHAPTER 10

What about the Romance, Where's the Joie de Vivre?

In my very long-lasting relationship and marriage to Mike, there have been many ebbs and flows. While I am proud of our relationship, it has not always been smooth sailing. You may recall it being said that, "Financial problems are the number one reason for divorce." I can attest that this problem can cause a relationship strain like nothing else. Particularly because financial lack causes uncertainty and uncertainty causes fear. I have shared with all of you that Mike and I fell on some very hard financial times around 2009, and it has truly taken about a decade to recover.

Through these years it has been difficult, even when you know someone so well, because everyone deals with fear and uncertainty differently. Communication for some (usually men) shuts down during times of extreme difficulty, and some (usually women) may tend to overexpress aiming to overcome the tension and worry. We were no different, and rather than throw the marriage away we decided to work on improving the financial situation and work through the day-to-day struggles with our relationship. Whether it is financial or any myriad of other problems that people go through in their marriages, at the end of the day only you and your spouse can decide if you want to put in the work or if the marriage is worth saving. Even in the best relationships, however, we need to constantly work on keeping it healthy if we expect to maintain it.

Midlife seems to be the time that many of us tend to be into our spousal relationships for about ten to fifteen years. You know, this is akin to being in our houses for ten or eleven years and we start to notice the paint chipping, the dishwasher breaking down, and we are having plumbing issues. To put it another way the bloom is off the rose. While it's true that many relationships break up at midlife, to say the least, at this time we become acutely aware of our partners faults. It's not to say that our relationships are the only cause for our possible angst and reflection but they certainly add to some of our pensiveness, contemplation, and reflection at this stage of our lives. Also, at this time, many of us have children, a mortgage, and so many responsibilities that the carefreeness and spontaneity of our early years together may seem like a faint memory. These days if we want to have the spontaneity of those early years, ironically, we need to pencil it in. Not only during this time do we neglect our own personal needs but unintentionally we sometimes neglect our significant other's as well. This can leave us feeling isolated and lonely.

What's more is it doesn't seem like our spouse "sees" us anymore. The little romantic gestures that used to be a part of our relationship seem to have vanished and have been replaced by the "practical" duties that need to be attended to on a daily basis. When the children come along, we know as good parents that our children's needs always come first. And by the time we have run the kids to soccer practice, cooked dinner, done the dishes, and thrown in a couple loads of laundry, the idea of romance at the end of the day can seem like a chore itself. How can we feel glamorous, romantic, and sexy when we have barely had time for anything but the day's chores?

A very funny yet somewhat realistic movie about this time of life is *This Is 40*. This is the story of a couple named Debbie and Pete who have been married for fourteen years and have two daughters—fourteen and eight years old. The movie starts out centering around the couple's fortieth birthdays. The only problem is Debbie does not want to be forty, so she won't admit it and claims to be thirty-eight.

In the opening scene the couple is making love in the shower, and through the steamed glass we can tell that they are enjoying it immensely; that is until Pete admits he took Viagra. Debbie then becomes extremely upset and shouts, "I am not forty and I don't have a husband that takes Viagra!" Pete does not understand why Debbie is so upset and he explains that he just wanted to "supercharge" their lovemaking. She says that she is highly insulted and doesn't want to make love to a man that needs Viagra to be sexually attracted to her. Debbie exclaims that she is not ready to be an old lady and needs two more years.

This incident upsets Debbie so much that she ends up talking to her personal trainer and girlfriend about it saying that she feels things have gone stale between her and Pete, hence the reason he is taking Viagra. The way these scenes are played in the movie are hysterically funny, and of course, we know that it is meant to be tongue-in-cheek, but part of the reason it is so funny is because it hits home. Any of us who have been in a long-term monogamous relationship know that it can be difficult to be consistently passionate. As time goes by each partner may have some difficulty with getting aroused from time to time, and even though this is perfectly natural, when it happens, we can't help but feel somehow our relationship is lacking or worse that our partner is no longer attracted to us.

The movie also hilariously points out how we notice all the little idiosyncrasies of our partner. In one scene Debbie confronts Pete with his habit of going to the bathroom four times a day for thirty minutes at a time. She bursts open the bathroom door to see what he is "doing in there." She sees that he is playing a video game, and she tells him he's got to stop "avoiding reality" by spending so much time in the bathroom. She then snatches the video game from his hands.

Another scene from the movie I really love is when Debbie and Pete go away for a weekend together alone. They are romantic and lovable with one another, they are not arguing and bickering like they do at home, and they reaffirm how much they love each other. Then, as soon as they pull up in the driveway the kids are running up to them shouting and fighting, and Debbie tends to them…and now we are home!

Other scenes that seem to hit home are the financial issues the couple are having. Peter has a record label business that he said he started because he could not find a job, and it is not doing very well financially. Additionally, he is giving his father money on a regular basis. Pete is keeping Debbie in the dark about much of the financial problems, and Debbie's retail store is $12,000 short and she suspects it is one of her employees that stole it. Then suddenly—without warning—oops we're pregnant again! Debbie waits a while to tell Pete and decides she will use an amorous gesture to talk about it that is completely wasted on him. This situation only seems to confirm, in Deb's mind, Peter's inability to find her sexually attractive.

I love the way the movie talks about some of the other things that pop up at this stage such as the need to forgive our parents and start taking responsibility for our own lives and actions. Another is cursing out loud and our kids picking up on it, and not sharing enough compassion and empathy with one another. Overall, the movie is a hilarious reminder of how life can get in the way of our ability to feel lovable, sexy, and fully alive sometimes.

It is probably true for most of us at this stage of life as moms, wives, daughters, sisters, and friends, and perhaps we are too busy to think of it, but as we move forward we come to the delicious ability to revisit some of the feelings of spontaneity, joy, tenderness, and empathy for ourselves as well as others.

Sometimes we can look at early midlife as if we are living someone else's life. Is this my life? How did I get here? We think our lives are so far from the "glamorous" life we envisioned. Particularly when times are hard, we may take a narrow view and feel we've let ourselves down. But we need to realize, if we haven't already, that loss and change are a part of life and the truth is we will always go through suffering.

Another thing that we are not seeing is the pressure we are under and how it can truly contract or "squeeze" the view of our lives. When we feel like the walls are closing in it's challenging to look at our lives from another perspective. There is no doubt there will be times in life for many of us that we need to make some changes in order to make our lives better. Beyond that, when I feel overwhelmed with the day-to-day pressures I play a bit of a game with myself— since I had some very rough years as a teenager, I think back to who I was or at least how I saw myself back then. Through my sadness, I virtually had no hope or expectation for myself back then. I then take an inventory of the blessings in my life along with my accomplishments and look at myself through the lens of that frightened and struggling young person that I used to be. You may say that you haven't experienced this type of trauma but the truth is no matter what the younger version of ourselves looked like you will be hard pressed not to amaze yourself by at least one of the accomplishments you have achieved since then. If that doesn't work try looking at your life through the eyes of a stranger. You know how we always look at our friends or neighbors and think that they have it made? Try doing this with yourself. The whole point is to take off the pressure and uncomfortable feeling you have right now and "take a new picture."

Once again, look at your life through a different lens. This may sound very simplistic or even silly at face value, but you will see that once you step out of the negativity or the "pressure cooker" you will have more appreciation for yourself and your life.

Another great movie that demonstrates our longing for the dreams we perhaps lost or maybe we feel we "settled" is *The Bridges of Madison County*. The main character, Francesca, is a woman who emigrated from Italy and came to the United States with her husband who had been a US soldier stationed in Italy during the war. She was thrilled to come to America but was now, at midlife, restless for the dreams she had that have been unrealized. When her husband Richard takes her two children—a son and a daughter—away for four days, Francesca meets a mysterious and intriguing photojournalist named Robert. Robert is doing a photo shoot around a major bridge within her small town in Iowa. One of the things about Robert that fascinates and irritates Francesca at the same time is the immense sense of freedom he enjoys. Being a traditional married woman with two teenage children and family obligations makes her realize that his life/freedom represents something that perhaps she at one time wanted or longed for herself. Admittedly, the life that she is living is not the life she dreamed of as a girl. Robert tells her that it is good to have had dreams, even if they didn't turn out the way we had hoped.

It is very clear to Francesca that Robert loves what he does and has great passion for it. Another thing that is clear is that she feels inferior to the "worldly" life and character he possesses. As the days go by they become extremely close, become lovers, and fall deeply in love. This is a love and feeling like Francesca had never experienced before. When Robert leaves he asks her to go with him. For a moment Francesca truly thought about leaving but knew that her responsibilities and obligations were to her family. The lovers would never see one another again but never forgot one another, and after Francesca's death her children read the story of her and Robert (left for them by Francesca). She also said that she wanted to be cremated and have her ashes thrown into the water over the bridge where some years earlier Robert had his ashes thrown when he passed. This was where Robert had taken pictures of the bridge as well as of Francesca.

Of course, Robert and Francesca had the perfect love because they would never be together. Had they gone off together eventually, Francesca's guilt would have been overwhelming, and it would have destroyed the love she had for Robert. Leaving her family was not something that she would ever do, so their love would always be perfect and untouched by the realities of life.

Love and relationship expert Esther Perel talks about the fact that suffering and pain are always part of life and therefore part of our relationships. That is why connection, intimacy, and empathy are so important. Esther says the reason that so many relationships today don't work is because we have too many choices and too few rules/boundaries and roles. Everything that was once a "rule" and part of a structure is now part of a question or a choice. Today, we have major expectations for a potential spouse; they must fulfill all our needs and they must make up for what we lack. Additionally, everything (including our spouse) needs to provide purpose and meaning. Needless to say, this is a very tall order. The question, "Who am I going to be?" is our main focus and we are incredibly "self" centered. Many of these types of notions take the place of formal religion. The relationships that are successful today seem to be much happier than successful relationships of the past—but are very rare—because it takes so much more today than it did in the past to be in a good relationship.

One of the many great points that Esther makes is that rather than have a laundry list of characteristics that we want in our spouse we should look for common values. Meet where both of your core values are—what can each of you both bring to the table to contribute and teach one another? There is no doubt the world is different today, and our relationships are changing along with everything else. As many of us may already know, choices are nice but there are definitely times in our lives where too many can be problematic. Unfortunately this seems to be a primary negative characteristic of our significant relationships as well.

The question we have to ask ourselves about our partnerships today is do we, as a couple, enhance the lives of each of us individually? In other words, what do we contribute to one another that no one else can? Those contributions and supports should always remain sacred and cherished. I think about the Bible verse from Mark 10:9, "Therefore what God has joined together, let no one separate."

While there are always many people in our lives that we love and care for including children, parents, relatives, and friends—and of course we always give them their place in our lives—there is always that sacred place that is just between us. I am surely not boasting, and I am well aware that relationships, like people, are always changing. But I have been with my husband (dating) since we were fifteen years old, and I can honestly say he holds a place in my heart that no one can replace.

The thing is my spouse and I are aware of this and we both work to keep precious the gifts that each of us bring to one another, and we are quite "stingy" and protective of them. It can be a great challenge to do this as we live in a world that is changing and there are so many challenges and responsibilities in everyday life, but there is always a part of me that only he can understand or comfort. My husband tells our now young adult children, "The trick is to find a spouse that vibes with your particular kind of weirdness." Nevertheless, as much as I love my partner, like Dr. Perel says, I also know that he does not, and cannot, fill all my needs.

Conclusion

———

If there is one thing I would like to make sure I have gotten across in this book, it is that life requires resilience, flexibility, and positivity. Yet, we all know that many things in life are not positive at all. No, I'm not advocating for rose colored glasses. I have not solved the puzzle of life, and my life is definitely not all unicorns and rainbows! I am no stranger to suffering the madness of what we call life.

I have my bad days like everyone else. There are times when I feel like a career-obsessed lousy mother and wife. While I know my way very well around the kitchen and do a great job of cooking and baking when I put my heart into it, I am not Martha Stewart when it comes to keeping an immaculate home. In fact, cleaning is one of my least favorite things to do around the house.

By now, the best thing about me is that I know these things about myself and there are no specific gender roles between my husband and me. In fact we have made alterations and compromises in our day-to-day lives to accommodate each of our strengths and weaknesses. On my best days I listen to what my heart, mind, and body are trying to tell me so that I can face the problem and know how to process and solve the issue. Sometimes we may have pain and we cannot determine where it is coming from. As we know, physical symptoms of problems/pain are often the result of an emotional issue that we are not wanting to look at. Our bodies, as we've talked about, are sometimes the first to tell us we're in need of some help.

There are times when the upfront emotional problems we feel stay in our consciousness too long and we need to do something about them. Just like physical ailments, we need to take care of ourselves and see the doctor. We need to do the same thing with our emotional well-being and take care of ourselves. I am a very firm believer in seeking professional advice and care when I need it.

I am a strong proponent of talking to someone about things that are bothering me. This can be my husband, a friend, counselor, or spiritual advisor. When my mom was alive, before she got sick and then passed away, we talked most days a few times a day. Sometimes she would just tell me her stories about the things that happened in her life. She would speak a bit of Italian, and I picked up many words from her Sicilian dialect. I would always talk to her about the people I knew, and she would always give me her insight. It's so funny because my sister will say, "I never knew that about Mom," or she'll say, "I don't remember her saying that." We laugh, and it's true—I don't think even my dad knew her as well as I did. But that's just because we talked so damned much!

I have never been able to replace the insightful advice she gave me on a regular basis. Since she has been gone, I have been working with spiritual advisors regularly. And when it comes to the point of needing to reach out for professional help (counseling) I am not afraid to do so.

While I am aware of the benefits of meditation, which I do from time to time, and understand there are great emotional and health benefits to yoga—which I don't practice—I do recognize that at times we need more than these things to assist with depression and anxiety that is spiraling out of control. And I am definitely a fan of modern Western medicine when it comes to taking medication. As a person who at a young age experienced a devastating depression, I know firsthand the benefits of taking these drugs.

However, I am also aware that in our society there is some major sense of shame associated with "needing" to take this kind of medication. The truth of the matter is that for the vast majority of people that take antidepressant or anti-anxiety medication, it is not a permanent thing (despite the rumors that it is permanent). And frankly for those of us that suffer from a chemical imbalance and need the medication permanently, the changes that one can experience as a result of taking the medication can be nothing short of life changing.

If I accomplish nothing else in this book, I want women to know that at this stage of life, we do have options. If you need support, ask for it. If you are not happy with your life, break down each part that you want to change and approach it one piece at a time. I strongly believe that anything can be done and anything can be accomplished with the right mind-set. I know this sounds simplistic, but I believe that this is true: life is 10 percent of what happens to us and 90 percent of how we respond to it. If nothing else, I hope that you will look at this book as a friend that is there to cheer you on to victory, and a comfort when you are having a hard time. Just remember, it takes a village, and we are in this together!

Acknowledgements

―――

I'd like to acknowledge those who have given this book, and the stories within them, legs strong enough to move forward.

Diana Padua, Monica Corley, Evelyne Fisher, Lisa Quick, Dorothy Tracy, Cynthia Forgue, Veronica Tracy, Cindy Tracy, Chloe Tracy, Beth Forgue, Karen Grogan, Kim White, Stacey D'Angeles, Michael Tracy, Eric Koester, Christine Morgan, Patricia Morgan, Becky Stenhaug, Jean Amos, Heidi Torres, Terri Nakamura, Lynda Condary, Cindy Jonke.

I'd also like to gratefully acknowledge

Ann Grogan, Nancy Kelly, Ann Lamp Thanos, Amy Wasiel, Jenny Yates, Michele Grogan, Kathleen Ellis, Maureen Bradford, Ryan Tracy, Ian Tracy, Bob Forgue, Jr.; Bryan Wish, Joel Gomez, Deidre Hammons, Tasslyn Magnusson, Miko Marsh, John Saunders, Brian Bies, Creator Institute, and New Degree Publishing.

Appendix

———

INTRODUCTION

Urbanska, Wanda. *The Singular Generation*. New York: Double Day Publishing, 1986.

CHAPTER 1 CHANGE YOUR MIND, CHANGE YOUR LIFE

Friedan, Betty. *The Feminine Mystique*. New York: W.W. Norton and Company, 1963.

.Kohn, Abby, Marc Silverstein, dir. *I Feel Pretty*. 2018; Burbank, CA: STX Entertainment 2018.

O'Connell, Catherine. "7 Powerful Tips for Finding Your Confidence at Midlife." Catherine Grace Co. Accessed October 1, 2021. https://catherinegraceo.com/wp-content/uploads/2019/07/My-7-Powerful-Tips-for-Finding-Your-Confidence-at-Midlife.pdf.

Salata, Shari. *TheBeautiful No: And Other Tales of Trial, Transcendence and Transformation*. New York:Harper-Collins Publishing, 2019.

CHAPTER 2 YOU'VE COME A LONG WAY, BABY

Collins, Gail. *When Everything Changed.* New York: Little, Brown and Company, 2009.

Dines, Gail and Jean M. Humez. *Gender, Race, and Class in Media.* California: Sage Publications, 2003.

Felsenthal, Julia. "The Author of Enter Helen on Why Helen Gurley Brown is Such an Enigma."*Vogue Magazine,* April 2016. https://www.vogue.com/article/enter-helen-brooke-hauser-interview.

Friedan, Betty. *The Feminine Mystique.* New York: Penguin Random House. 1963.

CHAPTER 3 HOW WE GOT HERE

Friedan, Betty. *Fountain of Age.* New York: Simon & Schuster, 1993.

Hoffman, David, and Carol Rissman. *Making Sense of the Sixties.* Alexandria, Va: PBS Video. 1990. https://www.youtube.com/watch?v=6UopH_PYlFU.

Raab, Diane. "Baby Boomer Women: A History of Empowerment." *The Huffington Post.* Updated May 9, 2015. https://www.huffpost.com/entry/baby-boomer-women-a-history-of-empowerment_b_6834854.

"What Is Gen X?" Corporate Finance Institute. Accessed October 7, 2021. https://corporatefinanceinstitute.com/resources/knowledge/other/gen-x/.

Chrisler, Joan C., andIngrid Johnston-Robledo. *Woman's Embodied Self: Feminist Perspective on Body and Image*. Washington, D.C.: American Psychological Association, 2018.

Doyle, Glennon. *Untamed*. New York: Penguin Random House 2020.

Dion, K., E. Berscheid, and E. Walster. "What Is Beautiful Is Good." *Journal of Personality and Social Psychology* 24, no. 3 (1972): 285–290. https://doi.org/10.1037/h0033731.

HealthyPlace Staff. "Eating Disorders: Body Image and Advertising."*HealthyPlace*. Updated May 30, 2017.https://www.healthyplace.com/eating-disorders/articles/eating-disorders-body-image-and-advertising.

"Generational Breakdown: Info about All of the Generations." The Center for Generational Kinetics. Accessed October 7, 2021. https://genhq.com/FAQ-info-about-generations.

Pipher, Mary. *Reviving Ophelia: Saving the Selves of Girls*. New York: Penguin House Publishing, 1994.

Pipher, Mary. *Women Rowing North: Navigating Life's Currents and Flourishing AsWe Age*. New York: Penguin House Publishing, 2019.

Raab, Diane. "Baby Boomer Women: A History of Empowerment." *The Huffington Post*. Updated May 9, 2015. https://www.huffpost.com/entry/baby-boomer-women-a-history-of-empowerment_b_6834854.

"2019 Statistics." Women and Hollywood. Accessed October 7, 2021. https://womenandhollywood.com/resources/statistics/2019-statistics/

CHAPTER 5 ACCULTURATION IN GIRLHOOD/YOUNG ADULTHOOD & CULTURAL BELIEFS/BODY IMAGE

Kilbourne, Jean. "'Killing Us Softly 4' - Key Points."*Women in the Social Sciences* (blog). April 17, 2013. https://history66kbcc.blogspot.com/2013/04/killing-us-softly-4-key-points.html.

Newsom, Jennifer Siebel, and Kimberlee Acquaro. "Miss Representation Discussion Guide." *Influence Film Club.* Accessed July 5, 2021. http://influencefilmclub.com/wp-content/uploads/2014/10/Miss-Representation-DG.pdf.

Doyle, Glennon. *Untamed.* New York: Penguin Random House, 2020.

Malacoff, Julia. "How Celebrity Social Media Affects Your Mental Health and Body Image." *Shape,* May 1, 2019. https://www.shape.com/lifestyle/mind-and-body/celebrity-social-media-affects-mental-health-body-image.

Meeker, Meg M.D. *Raising a Strong Daughter in a Toxic Culture.* Washington, D.C.: Regnery Publishing, 2019.

Pelley, Virginia. "What is the Divorce Rate in America? It's Complicated." *Fatherly.* Updated August 3, 2021. https://www.fatherly.com/love-money/what-is-divorce-rate-america/.

Thornhill, Ted. "Teenage Girl Killed Herself after Becoming Obsessed with Having a 'Perfect' Celebrity Figure and Taking Thousands of Pictures of Her Own Body."*Daily Mail*, November 24, 2015. https://www.dailymail.co.uk/news/article-3332113/Teenage-girl-killed-obsessed-having-perfect-celebrity-figure-taking-thousands-pictures-body.html.

Urbanska, Wanda. *The Singular Generation*. New York: Double Day Publishing, 1984.

"Youth and the Social Issues." *Youth in the 1980s* (blog). Accessed July 5, 2021. https://youthinthe1980s.weebly.com/social-issues.html.

Kay, Katty, and Claire Shipman. *The Confidence Code for Girls: Taking Risks, Messing Up, and Becoming Your Amazingly Imperfect, Totally Powerful Self.* New York: HarperCollins, 2018.

CHAPTER 6 EMBRACE THE CHANGES

Gilbert, Elizabeth. *Eat, Pray, Love.* New York: Random House Publishing, 2006.

Guardino, Christine M., Christine Dunkel Schetter, Julienne E. Bower, Michael C. Lu, and Susan L. Smalley. "Randomized Controlled Pilot Trial of Mindfulness Training for Stress Reduction During Pregnancy." *Psychol Health* 29, no 3 (November 2013): 334-49. https://doi.org/10.1080/08870446.2013.852670.

Huffington, Arianna. *Thrive.* New York: Random House Publishing, 2014.

Northrup, Christiane. *Goddesses Never Age: The Secret Prescription for Radiance, Vitality, and Well-Being.* New York: Hay House, 2015.

Northrup, Christiane. *The Wisdom of Menopause. 4th Edition.* New York: Penguin Random House Publishing, 2021.

Stanford Encyclopedia of Philosophy. s.v. "Marcus Aurelius." By Rachana Kamtekar. Accessed October 11, 2021. https://plato.stanford.edu/entries/marcus-aurelius.

CHAPTER 7 PERCEPTIONS AROUND WOMEN AND THE POWER OF MIND-SET

Garber, Megan. "When Newsweek Struck Terror in the Hearts of Single Women." *The Atlantic,* June 2, 2016.https://www.theatlantic.com/entertainment/archive/2016/06/more-likely-to-be-killed-by-a-terrorist-than-to-get-married/485171/.

Fonda, Jane. "Life's Third Act." Filmed November 2011 in New York, New York. TED Video, 11:20. https://www.ted.com/talks/jane_fonda_life_s_third_act.

TEDx Talks. "Patricia Katz: Light a Spark: Navigating the Mid Life Malaise." November 23, 2015. Video, 17:15. https://www.youtube.com/watch?v=UfvpJ6BCs9A.

Rauch, Jonathon. *The Happiness Curve: Why Life Gets Better after 50.* New York: Thomas Dunne Books. 2018.

Thomas, Pam, dir. *Sex and the City.* Season 3, episode 3, "Attack of the Five Foot Ten Woman." Aired June 18, 2000 on HBO.

CHAPTER 8 YOU GLOW, GIRL

Mawer, Rudy. "The Ketogenic Diet: A Detailed Beginner's Guide to Keto." *Healthline.* Updated October 22, 2020. https://www.healthline.com/nutrition/ketogenic-diet-101.

Brock, Kale. dir. *The Longevity Film: A Story about Living Happy, Healthy, and Disease Free. 2019.* Gravitas Ventures. 2019. El Segundo, CA.

Brown, Bobbi. *Beauty from the Inside Out: Makeup, Wellness, Confidence.*California: Chronicle Books LLC 2017.

Pelz, Mindy. "Keto and Menopause: Is the Keto Diet Helpful for Menopausal Women?" Dr. Mindy Pelz (blog). Accessed June 30, 2021. https://drmindypelz.com/keto-and-menopausal-women/

TEDx Talks. "Ann Phillippi: Why We Need to Disrupt Middle Age." August 20, 2018. Video, 15:32, https://www.youtube.com/watch?v=13pFXJ-GB7I.

Winfrey, Oprah. "A Transformative Conversation on Trauma, Resilience, and Triumph with Dr. Edith Eger." August 30, 2020. Video, 40:00.

CHAPTER 9 IT'S A SIDE HUSTLE WORLD

Lakhotia, Sanjay. "Gig Economy: A Boon for Women." *Entrepreneur,* May 24, 2019. https://www.entrepreneur.com/article/334272.

Sheppard, Maddie. "Women Owned Businesses: Statistics and Overview." *Fundera.* Updated December 16, 2020. https://www.fundera.com/resources/women-owned-business-statistics.

Unglesbee, Ben. "Who Really Killed Blockbuster?" *Retail Dive,* October 7, 2019. https://www.retaildive.com/news/who-really-killed-blockbuster/564314/.

Eisenberg, Richard. "Worth Watching: 55, Unemployed and Faking Normal." *Forbes,* August 3, 2017. https://www.forbes.com/sites/nextavenue/2017/08/03/worth-watching-fifty-five-unemployed-and-faking-normal/?sh=193b06d4737a.

CHAPTER 10 WHAT ABOUT THE ROMANCE, WHERE'S THE JOIE DE VIVRE?

Perel, Esther. "'Til Death Do We Part—Therapist Esther Perelon Relationships and Intimacy at End of Life." End Well. January 7, 2020. Video, 12:21. https://endwellproject.org/til-death-do-we-part/.

Eastwood, Clint. dir. *The Bridges of Madison County.* Universal City, CA: Amblin Entertainment and Malpaso Productions 1995.

Apatow, Judd, dir. *This is 40.* Universal City, CA: Universal Studios 2012.

Made in the USA
Monee, IL
15 June 2022

98080584R00085